Old Sanquhar Tales

A collection of folklore

compiled and edited by
Rog Wood

Illustrated by
Gary Bonn

First published 2010

© Publication Copyright Dumfries and Galloway Council
© Text Copyright Rog Wood

The right of Rog Wood to be identified as the author of this work has been asserted by him in accordance with the Copyright, Designs and Patents Act, 1988.

All rights reserved. No part of this work may be reproduced, stored in a retrieval system, or transmitted, in any form or by any means, electronic, mechanical, optical, photocopying, recording or otherwise, without the written permission of Dumfries and Galloway Libraries, Information and Archives.

Design, set and print by
Solway Offset *the* Printers, Dumfries
for the publisher, Dumfries and Galloway Libraries, Information and Archives

ISBN 978-1-899316-74-8

**Dumfries and Galloway Libraries, Information and Archives Central Support Unit,
Catherine Street, Dumfries DG1 1JB**

Foreword

Rog Wood has become one of Scotland's leading writers on farming and rural life in general. He has been the Scottish farming correspondent for Big Farm Weekly and Farmers Weekly and has written for many other specialist farming magazine, as well as regional and national newspapers. For nineteen years he wrote a weekly column for the Sunday Post under the pen name Tom Duncan and is currently the farming editor for the Herald writing daily news reports and a weekly column on Monday called Farmer's Diary. He is also the author of two very successful books called Magic Moments and Shepherd's Delight written under his pen name Tom Duncan.

This is his first venture into the mystical, yet intriguing world of folklore, combining it with some historical facts of life in Nithsdale. This lovely little book records some of the tales of witches and mysterious happenings in this area, passed down through the generations and are so ridiculous that they couldn't possibly be true... COULD THEY?

William Dalgleish

Rog Wood

Gary Bonn

Contents

Chapter 1	Douglas takes Sanquhar Castle	9
Chapter 2	Sanquhar Castle ghosts	13
Chapter 3	The Admirable Crichton	17
Chapter 4	Some queer stories of the old Tolbooth	21
Chapter 5	Town Pipers	29
Chapter 6	Crawick Mill Witches	33
Chapter 7	Apparitions near Sanquhar Manse	39
Chapter 8	Abraham Crichton's ghost	41
Chapter 9	The Ghost House	45
Chapter 10	The dreary Lady of the Linn	47
Chapter 11	Apparitions in Euchan	53
Chapter 12	The Ghosts of Littlemark and Dalpeddar	57
Chapter 13	Evil spirits at the Warld's En'	61
Chapter 14	The resurrectionist scare in Sanquhar	65
Chapter 15	Bryce's Loup	71
Chapter 16	Provost Whigham	77
Chapter 17	Olden hospitality in Nithsdale	81
Chapter 18	Burns and Black Joan	85
Chapter 19	The French prisoners of war and Lieutenant Arnaud	91
Chapter 20	Sanquhar fairs and the local wool trade	97

Acknowledgements for Old Sanquhar Tales

Reading old local books I became acutely aware that many wonderful folk lore tales were hidden amongst tedious history and genealogies of aristocrats. Victorian local authors tended to be ministers who wove a lot of their religious beliefs into their text and constructed complex sentences with words rarely used today. As a result, many modern readers would find it hard to persevere with reading these rare old books.

I therefore decided to collect the best of the old Sanquhar tales into one volume and to edit and rewrite them in a modern style. That way I hope these wonderful old tales will once again be read and enjoyed by a wide range of modern readers.

I therefore acknowledge the following original books from which most of the material for this book comes from. They are; Folklore and Genealogies of Uppermost Nithsdale by William Wilson; Annals of Sanquhar by Tom Wilson and W McMillan; Burns and Black Joan by T Wilson; Memorials of Sanquhar Kirkyard by T Wilson; History of Sanquhar by Rev. Robert Simpson; Traditions of the Covenanters by Rev. R Simpson; Chapels of Sanquhar by Rev. W McWilliam and Martyr Graves of Scotland by J H Thomson.

In addition I am indebted to Sanquhar's very own scribe, Willie Dalgleish and the Ewart Library's Graham Roberts, for their considerable help in proof reading and correcting the many mistakes I made. Finally, I must thank local artist Gary Bonn for his illustrations.

Rog Wood

Sanquhar Castle, circa 1880

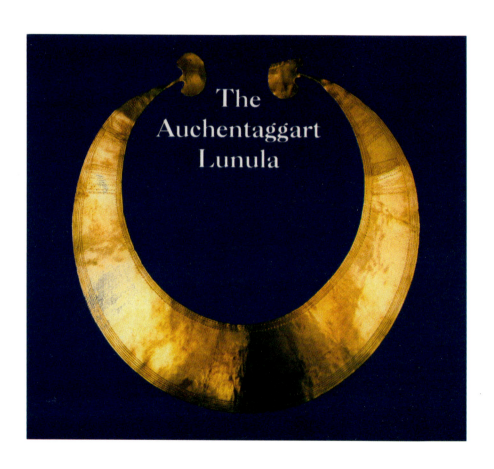

Chapter 1
Douglas takes Sanquhar Castle

Folk have lived in Upper Nithsdale for thousands of years and many ancient relics have been found in the area. Perhaps the most famous is a gold collar or torque called the "Auchentaggart Lunula", that was found on Auchentaggart Farm that overlooking Mennock from the east.

Auchentaggart means "fields of the priest" and probably got its name as a result of a nearby chapel at Dalpeddar. Before that, it may well have had some connection with ancient priests known as Druids. Nearby at Lochside Farm there was a crannog or lake dwelling on the Black Loch and a Druid circle on the hill of Knockenhair.

Anyway, in the winter of 1872-73, the lunula was found by John Wilson who was ploughman for T B Stewart, the tenant of Auchentaggart at the time.

When Wilson was dying, the doctor, J J Underwood noticed the yellow metal "collar" on the mantle and recognised that it was actually made of gold. He obtained the collar and gave it to the landlord, the Duke of Buccleuch, who passed it on to be displayed at the Royal Museum in Edinburgh. The collar is estimated to have been made between 2000 and 2500BC and is similar to collars worn by Egyptian pharaohs.

The name Sanquhar, or Sanchar as it was formerly spelt, is generally accepted as a compound of two Celtic words – Saen and Caer – signifying "old fort", pointing undoubtedly to the existence of an ancient British stronghold at the time of the Irish Scotia invasion in the ninth and tenth centuries. The site of this old fort is believed to have been the knowe immediately behind the present farmhouse of Broomfield, a few hundred yards north of the town.

The town of Sanquhar doubtless owed its origin to the existence of that fort. This was, indeed, the origin of many of the small country towns, both then and during the subsequent Anglo-Norman colonisation in the twelfth century. The people in those rough and unsettled times gathering for protection under the friendly shadow of a stronghold.

Another ancient fort of a later period lies immediately below the farmhouse of Ryehill in the form of a mote. There was a mote or meeting hill in every district of North Britain during an age when justice was administered to a coarse people in the open air. These motes belong to the Saxon age and were of two kinds – the folkmote and the witenagemot – an Anglo Saxon form of local parliament and place of assembly for the people where judgements were made.

In those rough times they proceeded with their business in an expeditious and unceremonious manner, and the unlucky person upon whom doom had been pronounced at the mote would have been found, in a short space of time, dangling at the end of a rope. The gallows for male and the pit for female offenders were the forms in which capital punishment was then administered.

The pit was filled with water, and the woman was put into a sack tied closely at the mouth, and then plunged into the pit so that her head was under water, where she was left until death put an end to her struggles. This was the power of "pit and gallows" possessed by the barons, and conferred by charter upon the civic authorities. Although the holders of such grim power clung tenaciously onto them, they were eventually taken from them by the abolition of heritable jurisdictions in 1748.

The exact date of the building of the most recent fortification, Sanquhar Castle, cannot be fixed, but there is no reason to doubt that it was the work of the Edgars or their predecessors in the twelfth century. In connection with the Anglo Norman colonisation in the reign of David the First, the first thing done by the colonists to defend the possessions the crown had granted them was the erection of a stronghold.

It does not appear the Normans obtained a very extensive footing in Nithsdale, the Irish Scotia, of whom the Edgars were, keeping their ground. There is no doubt the Normans' improved methods in building fortifications, as in everything else, would be noted by the native tribes. Anxious like their neighbours to keep their own, the Edgars set about building a stronghold becoming their rank and station, and of greater security than anything of the kind previously erected in the district. At all events, the castle is mentioned as being held by Richard Edgar during the reign of Robert Bruce.

The site of the castle was a well-chosen one. It was built on the verge of the plateau which runs along the valley of the Nith, overlooking what has once been the course of the river. It commanded the passage of Nithsdale, one of the lines of marching from England into Scotland, and was, both from its position and construction, a place of great strength. The possession of it was therefore, of great importance during the long lasting war between the two countries, and it frequently changed hands.

There is a tradition that towards the end of the thirteenth century, this stronghold was in the possession of the English, when all the castles at this time, from Carlisle to Ayr, were in the same occupancy. Captain Beufort, in the time of Wallace, kept this stronghold with a detachment of English soldiers, a matter that really upset the patriotic feelings of the inhabitants of the district.

In order to expel the intruders from the garrison, an urgent appeal was made to Sir William Douglas, one of our famous patriots, who readily accepted the request and lent his willing aid to regain the hold.

He collected his retainers and marching under the cloak of darkness, arrived unobserved within a short distance of the castle and hid his men close by the side of the Crawick – a spot familiarly called the witches' linn. Here in the gloom and silence of the trees, he waited his opportunity of making his descent unobserved through the wood, which at that time covered almost all the district.

The famous Dixon of Hazelside in Douglas Water – one of the faithful retainers of Brave Sir William – devised a scheme to recover the castle, which he successfully executed.

There was one Anderson who drove firewood to the castle from the neighbouring forest. Dixon did a deal with this man to achieve his objective. In addition to giving details of the strength of the garrison, Anderson agreed to swap clothes and let Dixon drive the cart with the wood to the castle in the morning. The men from Douglas were to follow Dixon warily in the half-light of dawn a short distance behind.

Accordingly when the carter got to the castle gate, he demanded admittance as usual. The sentry gave him a row for arriving so early, but as no deception was suspected, the very heavy portcullis was raised and the massive door on its grating hinges was thrown back. Dixon then drove forwards and firmly jammed the loaded cart in the entrance. On this Douglas and his men sprang over the wood, and stood within the castle gate. They instantly killed the sentry and then rushed in to the interior, running from one room to another they slaughtered the entire garrison with the exception of one man. He escaped by a back door and ran in breathless haste to Durisdeer, a neighbouring stronghold.

The news of the onslaught enraged the Durisdeer garrison and they rushed out, determined to take dreadful revenge on the daring band that had done so much harm to their countrymen.

It wasn't long till the castle was surrounded and a vigorous attempt was made to revenge the injury. It was all in vain, however, as Douglas defied them and stoutly held his position. The English, perceiving all their efforts in vain, decided to starve the defenders into surrender, and for this purpose regularly blockaded the fort. They persisted in this for two weeks, when Douglas sent a trusty henchman by the backdoor, who hastened to

Wallace, then in Lennox and asked for his help to rescue his friend the Douglas.

The Scottish patriot lost no time in rushing to the rescue, but when he was within a few miles the besiegers decided to retreat. As Wallace and Douglas pursued them the castles evacuated one after another in the line southward until they came upon the fugitives on the plains of Dalswinton. There a bloody fight ensued and five hundred of the English were left dead on the field. In this way the upper part of Nithsdale obtained a complete clearance of the invaders.

This event happened in the time of the chieftain Edgar, a number of years before it was occupied by the Crichtons. There is a wing of the old castle called "Wallace Tower" which respects the tradition that it was defended by the patriot on the occasion of an English attack. It is said that Wallace stood on the staircase in the inside of the tower and fought single-handed with the foe and defeating them before making his escape. This tower is the most entire part of the ruin.

Wallace defended Sanquhar Castle against the English

Chapter 2
Sanquhar Castle ghosts

Like many other old castles, Sanquhar Castle, or Crichton Peel to give it its alternative name, has its ghosts. Considering the many dark deeds that are said to have taken place within its walls, little wonder that there are stories of troubled spirits wandering to and fro among its ruined towers.

Two ghosts are said to haunt Sanquhar Castle – one male, the other female.

The male is said to be invisible, but makes its whereabouts known by loud groans and wailing and the rattling of chains. The female is a lady dressed in the white clothes she was buried in.

For their story we have to go away back to the days when the old barons were a law to themselves. Days when strength gave men the power to take what they wanted and rule others.

Stories have been handed down of folk being starved to death in the old keep and imprisoned within its walls until they had signed over to the greedy lords their rights to their possessions.

The disturbed spirit who makes his presence known by groaning and clanking chains is said to be that of an innocent man who was executed by Robert, the sixth Lord of Sanquhar. His name was John Wilson and he was both a tenant and servant of Sir Thomas Kirkpatrick of Closeburn.

The details of the arrest and execution of this innocent man are to be found in the Records of the Scottish Privy Council. It would appear from these that in 1597 Wilson had been sent by Kirkpatrick with a letter to Lord Sanquhar. As a sheriff he delivered the King's justice in Nithsdale and he had Wilson arrested and imprisoned in the castle.

At that time, Lord Sanquhar was friendly with his neighbour Sir James Douglas of Drumlanrig who had a quarrel with Kirkpatrick. Lord Sanquhar, apparently making his friend's quarrel his own, seized upon Wilson as a hostage for his friend Sir James.

Kirkpatrick complained to the Privy Council that under the pretext of justice, Lord Sanquhar intended a campaign of hatred and malice against Kirkpatrick's family, friends, tenants and servants. He also made a particular appeal for justice for poor Wilson and asked that he and his family and servants should be exempt from Lord Sanquhar's jurisdiction as sheriff.

That plea was granted by the Lords of Council, but Crichton resented their interference and in defiance of both them and the King had Wilson put to death by hanging on nearby Gallows Knowe. If traditions are correct, he wasn't by any means the only innocent man to meet his fate there.

The Gallows Knowe, or place of execution, was situated on the upper side of the main road between the Castle and Ryehill and is now cut through by the railway.

Beyond being suspended from his offices for a time, nothing whatever was done to Lord Sanquhar for his dastardly act.

Years after, however, his misdeeds found him out. In 1612 he was hung at Westminster for being accessory to the murder of Turner, a fencing master who had poked out one of his eyes by accident while they were practising with foils.

It was this Robert, Lord Sanquhar who in 1598 secured the Royal Charter for Sanquhar burgh.

Let us now return to the ghost. About 1830 a woman and her husband who had been out of the district for some time, returned to live in Sanquhar. They had great difficulty finding a house, but at last succeeded in getting a small one from the farmer of Castle Mains. The house, that had been used as a milk house and only had one room, no longer exists. It stood close to the ruins of the castle under the shadow of the old keep or Wallace Tower.

During the winter months that the couple lived in this lonely dwelling, they were greatly alarmed on several occasions by noises as if someone was going about the castle dragging a heavy chain. At the same time they also heard groans and sighs as if from a very distressed person. Although they searched on more than one occasion they were never able to account for the sounds and had no hesitation in putting them down to supernatural causes. Similar sounds have been heard by various people at different times.

The Lady in White was said to occasionally show herself, and her appearance was supposed to bode no good to the ancient Crichton family. She was the ghost of a beautiful maiden who had been seduced and cruelly murdered by one of the Lords of Sanquhar. She was only seen at rare intervals and when she did appear trouble was in store for the Crichtons.

Human remains have been found in and around the castle. A coffin was once found under the floor of one of the vaults that contained the skeleton of a tall, strong but headless man. On another occasion the skeleton of a woman, with long yellow hair still attached to the skull was discovered upside down in a pit or sewer. If the old walls could speak, what deeds of darkness they could tell.

There were also tales of an unknown apparition seen to the south of the castle, near the old Port Well, and also on the road between the castle and the ford through the Nith at what is now called the Old Mains. This was believed to be none other than Auld Nick himself.

Alexander Broadfoot of South Mains was a good-living, highly-respected man. He is said to have been attacked by the evil one in many disguises and ways, of which the following is an example.

He was a keen curler and had been in Sanquhar one night attending a meeting of fellow players in the Queensberry Arms Hotel. As there was extra business the meeting went on beyond its usual time.

Realising her husband was late, Mrs Broadfoot sent her daughter to the town on horseback to fetch him home. The business being at an end, Alexander mounted the horse with his stepdaughter getting up before him. Away they jogged down the street, past the castle and down the Port Well Brae to the ford.

The devil in the form of a large black wool sack terrified the horse

All went well until they reached the riverside. Just as they were entering the water the devil, in the form of a large black sack of wool, came rolling in before them and went floundering through the Nith, sometimes almost touching the horse's nose.

Broadfoot held his nerve and told his terrified companion to keep a firm grip of him and not to worry and, referring to God said, "There is Ane that has the care o' you and me this nicht, wha is stronger than a' the devils in hell".

When they reached the other side, the devil disappeared, but the horse, usually a quiet animal, snorted and shook with fear.

Finally there is the strange tale of William McCririck and William Cunningham who were tradesmen in Sanquhar. They had known each other a long time, had much in common and were good friends. For years they made a daily habit of having an after-dinner walk together, the Braeheads and Nithside being their favourite stroll.

Seldom was one seen without the other and only bad weather prevented their daily walk.

At last Cunningham fell ill and was confined to bed. His old friend McCririck was forced to have his walks alone. Each day on returning from his walk he called to see Cunningham who was making no improvement. Gradually he got worse and there seemed little hope of recovery.

After this had gone on for a few days, McCririck had been round the Braeheads, and at the south corner, where the Castle holm opens out, had stopped to admire the view down the valley.

Imagine his surprise when he saw Cunningham by the waterside below him, sitting on the bank near the little pool called the "Cradle". Unable to explain such an unexpected situation, he hurried down the steep bank towards his friend, who continued sitting in his characteristic position with snuff box on his knee. Coming within twelve yards or so of him, it turned out to be an apparition that vanished.

McCririck was amazed and something told him that his friend was dead. He speedily returned to the town and, on rounding the corner at the Council House was met by a fellow townsman who told him that William Cunningham had died a few minutes earlier.

At the exact time William McCririck had seen the appearance of Cunningham by the waterside, his old friend's soul was drifting into the great beyond.

Chapter 3
The Admirable Crichton

James Crichton, who became known as "The Admirable Crichton" was born on the 19th of August, 1560, at Eliock. He was the elder son of Robert Crichton, the Queen's Advocate and Laird of Eliock.

The Admirable Crichton was extremely handsome, whilst his accomplishments, both mental and physical, were almost superhuman and the talk of Europe. For over four centuries he has been looked on as one of the most wonderful men who ever lived.

While still a child, he was moved to Cluny in Perthshire and received his early education at Perth. He entered St Andrew's University when he was only nine years old and took his BA degree three years later. Two years after that, at the age of fourteen he became Master of Arts (MA). When he was fifteen, he was one of several youths who were chosen to assist by their companionship in the education of the young King James VI then aged nine.

He had mastered all the sciences and, besides his own, could write and speak fluently in ten different languages by the time he had reached seventeen, at which age he went abroad to improve himself by travel, as was the custom.

He went to Paris where he invited all comers to have a debate with him in any art or science to be carried on in any of ten specified languages, and either in prose or verse at the option of his antagonist. He gave the learned men six weeks to prepare for the contest. Meantime, confident of his own powers, he entered unrestrainedly into all the amusements and gaieties of Parisian life.

On the day appointed, in the presence of a huge audience, fifty masters in all departments of learning put to him the most intricate questions, to all of which he instantly responded with singular accuracy in the language they required. Four learned theologians next ventured to debate with him, but he refuted every argument they advanced. At the end, the president expressed their appreciation of his talents and scholarship, and amid the acclamation of all present, bestowed on him a diamond ring and a purse of gold. At the same time he saluted him with the proud title of "The Admirable Crichton".

After leaving Paris he spent two years in the French army. True to his Roman Catholic faith, he took part in the religious wars carried on by Henry III, fearlessly entering into the thickest fights and performing many acts of valour on many battlefields.

He was at Genoa in 1579 and there is a printed oration in Latin which he delivered on the first of July that year in the Ducal Palace at an election of the senate.

From Genoa he found his way to Venice, by this time in a condition of poverty. On his arrival he immediately addressed to Aldus Manutius, the great Venetian printer, a Latin poem in which he sought assistance. The Venetian archives record that at a meeting of the Council of Ten, held on the 19th August, 1580 (which, by coincidence was his twentieth birthday) his arrival was announced and chronicled in the following minute:- "There has arrived in this city a Scottish youth named James Crichton, who, as far as is known in regard to his social position, is of very noble birth, and who has been moreover, clearly proved to be possessed of the most rare and singular attainments by various trials and tests carried out by most learned and scientific men and particularly by a Latin oration delivered extempore this morning in our College, in such wise that he, though not past, or little past the age of twenty filled the minds of all with astonishment and stupor: a thing which, as it is in all points extraordinary and unlike what nature is accustomed to produce, has induced the Council to make some courteous demonstration in favour of this marvellous person, who, mainly owing to accidents which have happened to him and to vicissitudes of fortune is in very great straits, and, therefore, be it resolved that out of the funds of this Council there shall be handed to the aforesaid James Crichton, gentleman of Scotland, one hundred crowns of gold.

After staying in Venice for some months, ill and tired, Crichton went on to Padua. There was no rest for him there because amazing reports had gone before him. Despite his weariness he achieved his greatest triumph there.

The professors of the university gathered to honour him. On being introduced to them he improvised an excellent long poem in praise of the city, the university and the people present. After that he maintained a debate with them for six hours, and at its conclusion astounded everyone with an off-the-cuff eloquent speech on the bliss of ignorance.

Subsequently he offered to point out before the same university the errors in the philosophy of Aristotle, and to expose the ignorance of his commentators. He also refuted the opinions of certain celebrated mathematicians. It was all done in a common logical method, or by numbers or mathematical figures and by a hundred different kinds of verses. He performed this stupendous task before a big audience, whom he held spellbound for three days. This amazing feat was finished amidst deafening shouts of applause that, said one writer, "nothing more magnificent had ever been heard by human ears".

"The Admirable" next continued his progress to Mantua, arriving there at a time of much excitement over the deeds of a professional gladiator. He was a man of extraordinary powerful physique and an expert swordsman who had foiled some of the best fencers in Europe. He had previously killed three gentlemen of the court of Mantua who had recently fought against him and whose deaths were greatly deplored. This swordsman had now challenged all and sundry to a combat for a stake of 1500 pistoles, the currency at that time.

Crichton at once took up the challenge and fearlessly encountered his antagonist. At first acting on the defensive he suddenly went on the attack, and with so much dexterity and vigour that with three thrusts he ran him through the body in three different places, killing him on the spot. With characteristic generosity he gave the prize money to the widows of the men the gladiator had slain.

Struck with this splendid exhibition of courage and skill, not less than with his mental talents, the Duke of Mantua took Crichton into his service in February 1582.

He became the Duke's friend and chief adviser and drew up a plan of fortification for him. He also became a dramatic writer and actor and composed a comedy in which he exposed the vices and ridiculed the weaknesses of the different occupations in life, he himself playing fourteen different characters in succession. He instantly gained the admiration of the people of Mantua, was especially loved by the ladies, was fawned on by courtiers and praised by men of learning. All this roused the jealousy of Prince Vincenzo Gonzaga, the Duke's son and heir who had been accustomed to rank first in popularity. He fostered an intense hatred of Crichton and secretly plotted to put him out of the way.

So it came about that during the festivities of Carnival on the night of 3rd July, 1582, as Crichton wandered the streets he was attacked by three masked men – the prince and two hired assassins. With his usual skill he dispersed his assailants, killing one and disarming the leader, whom he recognised. So strong was his sense of loyalty that he immediately dropped on his knee and offered his sword to Gonzaga, who cowardly thrust him through the body. It was a dastardly and cruel deed. Crichton's tragic end led to widespread grief and detestation of the cowardly prince.

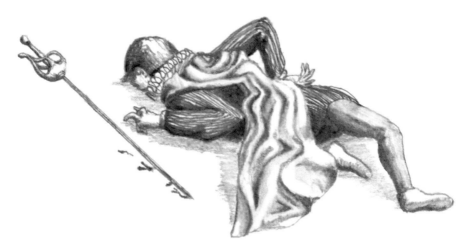

The Admirable Crichton was run through with a sword

Crichton's body was taken to the house of a chemist. The Duke, hoping that the scandal involving his son would be soon forgotten, didn't order the last rites of the church to be given for the body. The chemist refused to keep the body longer, so Crichton's servants, who had no money, placed it in a tarred coffin, and on the 5th July, under cover of night, the Admirable Crichton was buried in the neighbouring church of San Simone – a melancholy end of the most brilliant career.

The lands of Eliock and Cluny that the Admirable Crichton did not live to enjoy were inherited by his brother, Sir Robert Crichton. He was a lawless and unprincipled waster, who in a few years lost everything.

Chapter 4
Some queer stories of the old Tolbooth

Sanquhar Council House or Tolbooth was built in 1735 to a design by the famous architect William Adam and replaced an older two storey one that had been thatched with heather but had become dilapidated by 1680.

The present building is made of stones taken from Sanquhar Castle when it was partially dismantled by the Duke of Queensberry.

The outside stairs lead to what was the council chambers and courtroom, beneath are the old cells and on the south side a room that was used as a school. A room above the council chamber, which is accessed from the clock tower, was used to imprison debtors.

Three of the cells were fitted with fireplaces – the debtors room and the inner cells under the courtroom, but in the "Thief's Hole" – the name given to the double cell on the ground floor beneath the tower – no such comfort was given. It must have been a cold miserable place and it was only used for prisoners who had committed the worst offences.

Unlike overcrowded modern prisons the cells often stood empty. During one of the periods of famine that were common at the close of the eighteenth century, two cells were fitted up as a meal market to supply oatmeal at a cheap rate to the townsfolk, many of whom were starving.

The cells were redundant by 1840 when the town started sending wrongdoers to the county prison in Dumfries.

The last record of prisoners being held in the Tolbooth was in the 1880's when the police lock-up was being altered and the "Thief's Hole" was temporarily used to detain prisoners.

Fixed to the Tolbooth wall by the side of the prison door at the corner facing down the High Street, is an upright iron bar or staple on which is a strong iron ring. This is known as the "jougs" and like the English pillory and stocks was used to punish those guilty of petty thefts.

An iron chain attached to the ring was put round the neck of the prisoner and padlocked. That way the townsfolk could punish the offender with gibes and insults, or even pelting them with rotten eggs and other offensive missiles.

The "Jougs"

Typically, when an offender was to be punished by public exposure the sentence of the court was generally so many days imprisonment with two hours each day in the jougs.

The practice was last enforced about 1830.

Another degrading punishment was given to female offenders. They were taken out of the prison with a rope round their neck to be led by the jailor. On their back was pinned a notice that declared "This is a Thief".

As she was led through the burgh and back again, a man followed behind beating a drum to draw attention.

Local folk long-remembered one good looking young woman being punished this way in the early 1820's. The annual bonspiel between Sanquhar and Kirkconnel was being played that day at Sanquhar. As the Kirkconnel curlers came down for the game one cold, frosty morning at about 10 o'clock they saw the young woman being led out of the Council House. After her humiliating walk of shame she was banished from the burgh.

Most would reckon the Tolbooth was a secure prison, but at different times some escaped.

One notable escape was made about 1820 by a woman called Kirsty McLean, a homeless vagrant who went about the countryside as a hawker. She slept in farm outhouses and was well known all over Upper Nithsdale.

At the time of the story she was lodging at "The Holm", a farm near Leadhills, where she had lodged before. As a result she had got to know every nook and corner of the house and among other things learned where her host kept his money. Kirsty stole it and made off before the family awoke.

The loss was soon discovered, and as Kirsty was the number one suspect a chase was made that led to her being caught and imprisoned in the Tolbooth to await trial.

Hanging was the punishment for such a crime in those days and her fate seemed sealed. Most would have thought it impossible to break out of the Thief's Hole, where she was locked up, but Kirsty didn't like the thought of being hung and set her brains to work.

After she had been detained for a week she pretended to be sick and one evening persuaded Robert Dargavel, the jailor, to let the door between the day cell and the sleeping cell to be left open, saying she might need to go into the day cell before morning.

Kirsty changed places with the jailer

Accepting her plea, Dargavel didn't lock her into the sleeping cell that night, so she had the run of both places, and after locking the outside door for the night, he left her.

Next morning Dargavel came at the usual time to give Kirsty her breakfast. Opening the outer door, he saw that the door of the inner cell was closed. Concluding that his prisoner was still asleep, he left the key in the outside lock and went forward with the intention of wakening her. No sooner had he done so than Kirsty, who was standing behind the outer door, rushed out. Before he could get to her she had closed the door and turned the key, changing places with her jailer. Kirsty slipped the key in her pocket, watched her opportunity and made off.

Dargavel was kept a prisoner in his own jail for some hours. Meanwhile his wife, wondering what had become of him, left her home to look for him. After finding him in his predicament she was heard to exclaim to some bystanders, "Sirs, Robert's here, but Kirsty's away". A locksmith had to be brought to set him free.

The minutes of the town council recorded that, "for his gross fault and neglect" in allowing Kirsty to escape, Robert Dargavel was sacked from his post of town officer and jailer. Shortly afterwards, however, he was reinstated.

As for Kirsty, despite searching all over she was never found. No doubt she had been concealed by some kind-hearted person who did not wish to have her hanged, as doubtless she would have been had she been brought to trial.

After about ten or twelve years, when the person she had robbed and the principal witnesses were dead, she came back on her rounds as she had done before and often entertained the Sanquhar folk with the story of how she tricked the jailer.

As mentioned earlier, there was a fireplace in the inner cell under the courtroom, and in cold weather prisoners were allowed a fire.

On one occasion, about 1840, this nearly led to a fatal result. Henry Wright had stolen some percussion caps from a shop belonging to a Mr Halliday and was committed to jail. As the weather was cold, they lit a fire for him.

He was locked up in that cell with the window that looks on the stairway. By some means or other the straw of the bed caught fire and the place quickly filled with smoke.

Wright was in danger of being suffocated. He held his face out between the bars of the window to get fresh air and his shouts soon drew people to his assistance, who then threw pails of water into the cell to put the fire out.

Fortunately there was no fear of Wright burning as there was scarcely anything beside the straw to burn. However, to be doubly sure his friends outside dashed plenty of water on him so that if there wasn't a risk of being burned he certainly had a narrow escape from being drowned.

All this time Wright was in this woeful plight, the jailer was away doing something elsewhere and had the key of the prison in his pocket.

When Wright's trial came he got off lightly on account of the fright he had. He went on to lead a vagabond life all his days and caused much expense and annoyance to the local authorities before he died in Dumfries Asylum in 1888.

A ludicrous story is told of the debtor's prison, the cell under the roof of the tower. William Stitt from Durisdeer was unfortunate enough to get into debt with an unmerciful creditor, and this led to his detention in Sanquhar jail.

The debtor's room was not uncomfortable, but the few bedclothes provided were poor. Being in the dead of winter, and a hard frost on the ground, Stitt ran a pretty fair chance of freezing to death.

To prevent that happening he decided to make an attempt to get more blankets. One night he managed to force his way through the skylight

Tolbooth and Public Hall, Sanquhar, 1896

window in the roof. He then descended to the street by means of an old smithy, which at that time and for many years after, stood close to the wall at the back of the Council House.

After his escape he went home to Durisdeer and got some blankets before returning to Sanquhar. When the jailer came in the morning he found Stitt waiting to be let in with a bundle of blankets on his back. "The nichts were gey cauld", he said, "an' he thocht he wad be daein' nae harm, an' never be missed sud he step awa' hame for some claes to keep him warm."

This escapade of Will Stitt resulted in his liberty, for his creditor hearing of the exploit refused to press charges, and so he was set free.

Horse and Carriage, Queensberry Square, Sanquhar, circa 1880

High Street showing the Cameronian Monument

Chapter 5
Town Pipers

The Town Piper played an important role in many Scottish burghs in the past and was a person of considerable importance.

The duty of Sanquhar's piper in the eighteenth century was to walk the burgh every week-day morning at 6 o'clock and in the evening at seven. His services were requested on all occasions of public celebration and indeed no festivities were reckoned complete unless accompanied by a piper.

His reward was clothing and a small salary out of the public funds. In addition he enjoyed certain privileges, the main one being the right to seek the goodwill of householders who felt bound to pay him a small amount each year depending on their circumstances.

The piper was always present at births, christenings and weddings and was a welcome guest at many of the farmhouses. There he supplied music at celebrations and frequently entertained workers in the harvest field.

The cheerful skirl of the pipes sounding up the street helped to cheer up the homes of the townsfolk.

Pipers were notoriously thirsty and Sanquhar's were no exception. Their opportunities for indulging were many. In those days when mirth and whisky went hand in hand, it's little wonder that many became alcoholics.

His fondness for a dram led to the death of one of Sanquhar's Pipers. It occurred during the days of the Covenanters. The piper had been at some party at a distant farmhouse. His way home led him through the Sanquhar Muir, of which Lochside Farm is part of, and he was very much under the influence of drink.

A company of soldiers happened to be on the Moor at the time in pursuit of a Covenanter who was known to be hiding in the moss hags. As the piper neared the Black Moss he stumbled and fell, when the soldiers, thinking he was the fugitive trying to hide, shot him.

When the soldiers realised their mistake they were very upset because the piper was well-liked, having skirled through the burgh for many years.

His body was carried down to the town, and in order to show their respect for an old friend, all the soldiers garrisoned at the Castle followed the corpse to the grave. The Duke of Queensberry himself was one of the mourners.

A heap of stones was raised by the soldiers and became known as the "Piper's Cairn".

One of the last of the old-style official pipers of Sanquhar (as opposed to the modern day ceremonial pipers) was a great worthy. He had the misfortune to be married to a quarrelsome, scolding shrew of a woman. The manner of her burial is both remarkable and disgraceful.

The piper was a merry, good-natured soul, fond of a dram, could sing a good song and tell a queer story. In other words he was the very life and soul of a good party. He was also a good player, so his presence was essential at weddings and other parties.

Merry and light-hearted, he was a welcome guest at every house save one and that was his wife's! Solomon said, "A continual dropping in a very rainy day and a difficult woman are alike".

In regard to the piper's wife the words of the wise king were substantially correct. She was a peevish, discontented woman who was never at rest and seemed to take delight in making all unhappy who were unfortunate enough to go within hearing of her sharp tongue.

For many years the poor piper lived a wretched life with her, often cursing the day that he married her.

Death however, at last relieved him of her and came so suddenly and unexpectedly that the event quite overpowered him.

His friends and acquaintances went to console or rather to congratulate him and with drinking and merriment they passed the time between death and burial.

On the night before the day fixed for the burial an extra lot of liquor was brought in to properly celebrate the "kistin" (wake) and before long the mirth and fun were going well.

Some of the lads had brought their girlfriends with them and they started to dance. Unfortunately the house was small and the coffin took up most of the room available for dancing.

This obstacle to their enjoyment was soon resolved. The grave was already dug: why not bury the corpse at once? No sooner said than acted upon, and in the grey dawn of a summer morning the funeral took place.

The piper, dressed in all his paraphernalia, took his place at the head of the coffin and, followed by the company in pairs, played a merry quickstep up the street.

The piper played a merry quick tune

The sound of the pipes at such an unearthly hour raised the townsfolk from their beds to a sight they never forgot.

The coffin was carried shoulder high by four young men and the piper never stopped playing until they reached the kirkyard. After lowering the coffin, he then took up the pipes and continued to play until the last spade of earth had been thrown into the grave. The company then returned to his house and the scandalous ceremony ended in drunken disorder.

The piper never remarried but continued to live alone until his death at a very old age. A story is told of how on a wild night the thatch on the roof of his house began to be blown off by the violence of the storm. His neighbours woke him up to tell him the danger his house was in. "A' weel" was his indifferent reply, "If the win' has blawn aff the roof, the win'll just have to blaw't on again," and went back to sleep. He of course meant the wind of his bagpipes, and the money he earned from playing them would pay for repairing the roof.

Crawick Village, circa 1900

Crawick Bridge, circa 1932

Chapter 6
Crawick Mill witches

From the earliest of times and in many countries people have believed in the existence of witches, wizards and sorcerers. Such strange beings, working in hand with the Devil, were supposed to be able to alter the course of nature's laws. Helped by Satan's power, they used glamour, charm and spells to cast terror and hurt their neighbours. They were capable of all kinds of mischief and wickedness against those unfortunate enough to have fallen foul of them.

It wasn't just the poor and ignorant who were superstitious, all kinds of people throughout the land believed in such things.

Laws were passed that condemned hundreds of innocent people to be horribly tortured for imaginary crimes and the alleged use of powers they never possessed.

In Scotland, as elsewhere, the belief in witchcraft was universal. By the time Queen Mary ruled Scotland, nearly every accident or disease that befell man or beast was blamed on some old man or woman who had the bad luck to be suspected of having dealings with the Devil.

Things got so bad that an Act was passed in 1563 that allowed suspected witches to be tried and if found guilty, to be burned at the stake.

The Act was vigorously enforced with the Government hiring a number of paid officials called witch-finders whose job was to find and bring to trial all those suspected of dealing in the black art. This was the cause of many a poor innocent old person being accused and brought before the authorities. They were often condemned to be burned at the stake without even a proper trial.

Dumfries had its full share of anti-witch mania and in April 1659 no less than nine women were burned at the stake in one day at the burgh's execution place. It's an awful thought!

Any peculiarity in manner or appearance shown by an old woman was enough to brand her as a witch. Friendless and already suffering from old age and poverty she was subjected to inhuman treatment.

A minister of Kirkbride near Kirkconnel, the Rev. Peter Rae believed that a woman had bewitched him, and had her cut across the brow in order, as he supposed, to prevent any bad effects resulting from her spell. The cut across the brow – "abune the witch's breath" – was done with a sharp knife, and was called the "witch's score".

About that time a lot of witches were found and the executioners were kept busy.

The last execution for witchcraft took place in 1722, when a poor Highland woman was burned at Dornock. Even as late as 1805 the Procurator Fiscal of Kirkcudbright thought it necessary to prosecute a woman for witchcraft. She was sentenced to a year in prison and once every three months, on a market day, to stand openly in the "jougs" at Kirkcudbright's market cross.

The village of Crawick was well-known for witches, and appears to have been a sort of headquarters for the sisterhood. Their antics were talked about locally and far and wide. Many tales were told of meetings at the "Witches Stairs" – a huge rock among the linns of Crawick. There in the company of other witches from all over the country, they planned their evil deeds and cast their spells to hurt those they didn't like.

Sometimes the farmer's best cow would stop giving milk, a mare wouldn't have a foal, or the churn would be spellbound, and churn again, but no butter would come.

The Manse of Sanquhar at that time was situated close to the river on the site now occupied by the Blackaddie House Hotel, and the minister who lived there was afflicted by just such a churn. He told his servant girl to carry the churn to the other side of the Nith, thinking that crossing a running stream would break the spell. That didn't work but neither did fixing a rowan tree branch in the byre, nor nailing a horse shoe behind the door.

The power of the witch was too strong for the minister, but his wife was more successful. She made up a nice roll of butter from a churning she had done earlier and along with a big jug of milk, gave it as a present to the witch at Crawick suspected of casting the spell. The gift was thankfully received and the churn worked well from then on.

The miller at Crawick Mill was an honest, well-respected, popular man called Robert Stitt. One day, however, he refused to give one of the Crawick witches a small amount of meal. She was enraged at the refusal and told him "he would rue that ere mony days passed".

About a week afterwards on a dark night, Crawick was in full flood. The miller went to put down the sluice, missed his footing, fell into the water, was carried off by the torrent and drowned.

Another tale concerned a young man who started out early one morning to go a journey. Shortly after setting off he met one of the witches, when some words passed between them. She said to him, "Ye're gaun briskly awa' my lad, but ye'll come riding hame the nicht". The poor chap broke his leg that day, and was brought home in a cart as the witch predicted.

An old woman called Nannie is said to have been the last of the uncanny crew that dwelt on the banks of the Crawick.

She appears to have been very intelligent and knew that she was considered a witch, an idea she encouraged. That kept her neighbours in awe and also helped her to get a living. The ignorant and superstitious gave her lots of presents so she would think well of them and not put them under her spells.

One fine summer's day she was standing at her door smoking her pipe and enjoying the scenery when Jock, "a de'il of an ill callan", and leader in all the mischievous pranks in the village, came briskly by. Running up to her he snatched the pipe out of her mouth and threw it to the ground, at the same time telling her that, "witches had nae richt to smoke". Nannie replied, "O, Jock, ye'll sodger yet". She had been impressed by his daring, as all the other boys were quiet and subdued when near her. Nannie's words came true. Jock became a soldier and died fighting for his country in the French wars.

The surprising thing about the Crawick Mill witches is that none was ever caught at a time when so many were put to death in other parts of the country. It may have been that the witches of Crawick Mill were too cute for the witch-finders, having a handy habit of transforming themselves into cats, dogs and hares, and taking to the fields when danger was near.

Here is an instance. A man going through the fields one day with his gun in search of game saw a hare run past him. He fired and hit it just as it entered a wood, the shot making the fur fly from its hips.

He followed on, expecting to find the dead hare, but could see no trace of it. Instead he saw behind a bush one of the Crawick Mill witches sitting picking shot out of her body!

It appears the witches were interested in curling matters and lent a hand to those they wished to win.

As far back as 1760 the curlers of Crawfordjohn were in the habit of playing a game with the curlers of Sanquhar. At the time of the story the Crawfordjohn curlers had been unsuccessful for a year or two and, according to custom, had to come to Sanqhar to play.

They had to leave home early in the morning to be in time for the day's sport and arrived at Crawick Bridge in the grey light of the winter morning. As the first of their party was crossing the bridge they saw a hare run by and this was seen as a bad omen. One of the party exclaimed, "O, men

The hunter found one of the Crawick Witches picking shot out of her body

we'll lose the day. See thae infernal witches are at their pranks again". Sure enough, they lost!

The following year, as the Crawfordjohn men were coming down from Crawick, all determined to do their best, and no doubt feeling anxious as to the result of the day's play, who should they meet but one of the Crawick Mill witches!

This was an opportunity that they were determined to make the most of. Mindful of the defeat they supposed the witches to have caused them to suffer they surrounded her and forced her to spit on each of their broom brushes as a protection against any spell that might be cast against them.

The protection that gave them worked. That day the Crawfordjohn men were victorious. The following winter, on the 24th January, 1776, the Sanquhar curlers had to travel to Crawfordjohn.

The contest was at Duneaton Water and the Sanquhar men were the victors. This was among the last games between the two parishes. No doubt the curlers of Crawfordjohn saw the futility of trying to beat the men from Sanquhar who were backed by witchcraft!

There was an old man, a Mr McMichael of the Gavels, which is now part of Tower farm, who was terribly annoyed by fairies and witches who he believed brought him much harm.

One summer night he went outside to pray, but as he drew near his usual spot he saw, on the green grass beneath an old oak tree a large number of fairies dancing in a ring, accompanied by fine music. They were all dressed in green with red caps and each one looked like a little prince or princess.

He rushed back to the house and told the rest of the family to come and see the grand sight, but when they returned to the place they had disappeared.

One time all his milk went sour and no one was able to explain why. At last it was decided that witchcraft was the cause, but in spite of all the potions and charms used, the spell remained unbroken.

Old McMichael, driven to his wits' end, went to the minister to explain what had been happening, telling him which of the Crawick Mill witches he suspected.

When the minister had heard his story he gave him the following instructions. First, he was to go home and take all the milk that was left in the house, and having made sure that none was left, put it into a large pot and set it on the fire. He had also to see that all his milk dishes were thoroughly cleaned in hot water.

Next, a man had to set off on horseback to the house where the suspected witch lived and take a piece of divot from any part of the roof except the east corner. Once this was done, to gallop back as quickly as possible and put the horse in the stable.

Into the divot taken from the witch's house a pin was to be stuck for every cow that McMichael possessed and then put into the pot of milk boiling on the fire.

Another divot was to be placed on the top of the chimney, the windows all screened and the door locked. The entire household was to remain indoors with the exception of a boy who was to look out for the witch coming, as come she would, and in great pain because for every bubble made by the boiling milk she would feel as if a pin had been stuck in her.

On no account, however, was she to be let into the house unless she repeated the Lord's Prayer correctly. If she did that the spell would be broken, cows and milk would all be made right and she herself freed from her torture.

These instructions were fully carried out and a sharp boy, called James Halliday, was sent to the top of a knowe, a short distance from the house, to watch for the coming of the witch.

He didn't have long to wait, for in a short time he saw her coming directly from Crawick Mill running as fast as she could. She was soon at the door and evidently in great distress cried out to be let in. She was informed that admittance would only be allowed after she had correctly repeated the Lord's Prayer.

This at first she refused to do, but finding all efforts for admission fruitless she made an attempt at the prayer and began by saying, "Oor taither which wart in heaven". She continued the words in this style but was plainly told that unless she repeated the words correctly and in a proper manner she would not get into the house.

All this time the milk was boiling on the kitchen fire and the witch appeared to be in agony.

At last, unable to hold out any longer, she repeated the prayer properly and was then allowed to enter. She immediately ran to the fire and took off the pot, breaking the spell. The witch got immediate relief from her pains, the cows and milk did well ever after and McMichael was never troubled with witches again.

Then there was the tale told by the farmer of Ulzieside, known as a God-fearing man who was often troubled by the Devil and his helpers.

It was his custom to retire to a quiet place near a well to meditate and pray. One calm, dark night, near the end of harvest, he was at his devotions when Satan went past him playing on the bagpipes. Behind the Devil followed a large number of witches and warlocks linked together in pairs.

The farmer was very afraid and prayed that God would take care of him. As soon as the name of God passed his lips the weird company went away in flashes of fire, like forked lightning, darting in every direction and making the glens of Euchan ring with their eldritch yells.

Chapter 7
Apparitions near Sanquhar Manse

From time to time a mysterious apparition was seen near Sanquhar Manse, now called Sanquhar House. The place haunted doesn't appear to be the Manse itself, but that part of the glebe next to the public road. It was also seen on the avenue and roadway between the Manse and the kirk.

Some folk reckoned that the ghost that haunted this area was somehow connected with the ancient, tree covered mound close to the Manse and associated with the Druids. Whatever may be the cause, there was no doubt that uncanny beings were frequently seen there, as several folk could testify.

A Mrs Hamilton of Castle Street told a story of how one Sunday afternoon, about 1850, she and a friend visited a Mr and Mrs Hislop at the Tower Farm. The Hislop's two children were suffering from scarlet fever at the time.

Mrs Hislop was keen for them to keep her company as long as possible and pressed them to stay until after nine o'clock when they finally left for their homes in Sanquhar. It was a bright, moonlit night, fine and calm with everything still.

At Whitehill they were joined by Mr Orr, the parish schoolmaster, who started chatting with them and accompanied them towards the town. They were walking along quietly until when within fifty yards or so of the avenue to the Manse all three were startled by the sudden and mysterious appearance of a man a few yards in front of them, right in the middle of the road.

His appearance was so sudden that he seemed to have risen out of the ground. His feet made no sound and he appeared to glide along rather than to walk in front of them.

The three were struck by terror as they were certain it was no mortal walking on in front of them. Without saying a word they took a firm grasp of each other's hands and felt impelled to follow the mysterious apparition. It continued to glide along until it reached the avenue to the Manse, when it disappeared as suddenly and unaccountably as it had appeared.

The three were amazed at such an inexplicable event and Mr Orr tried for a long time to find an explanation of the mystery, but it remains unsolved to this day.

A similar apparition was seen by a Mr David Oliver and a friend who were out for a walk before going to bed. It was also a nice, calm evening, dark, but not particularly so.

While walking and quietly chatting the appearance of a tall, dark man sprang up beside them, near a clump of trees that marked the glebe boundary. It also glided along noiselessly, keeping step with Oliver and his friend until they came to the avenue to the Manse, where it vanished. It made no noise whatever, nor did it speak, or try to interfere in any way with either of the two friends.

This same apparition has been seen in the roadway between the avenue and the Broomfield and also between there and the Kirk. A white ghost has also been seen in the glebe between the Manse and the Milestone.

It will be remembered that the ghost of Abraham Crichton often showed itself in the fields near the kirkyard frightening milkmaids. Therefore the area between the kirkyard and the glebe has always had a kind of uncanny reputation that required a lot of bravery to walk through after dark.

Kirkbride

Chapter 8
Abraham Crichton's ghost

The story of the ghost of Abraham Crichton, that haunted the kirkyard of St Brides in Sanquhar, is one of the best known of Sanquhar's traditional ghost stories.

Abraham Crichton was a merchant in Sanquhar. He was a descendant of the ancient lords of Crichton Peel and lived at his place of business in the High Street.

He was a shrewd, active businessman, reputed to be very wealthy and well thought of. In 1734, on the death of his brother, Provost John Crichton, whom he succeeded as laird of Carco, the townsfolk made him the chief magistrate.

He took a keen interest in the welfare of the burgh and during his term of office they began to build the Council House.

Abraham's prosperity didn't last and in 1741 he was declared bankrupt. Some years before, the parish of Kirkbride had been merged with the neighbouring parishes of Sanquhar and Durisdeer and the ancient kirk was allowed to fall into a state of disrepair.

The former members of the old kirk had to go to the rebuilt kirk in Kirkconnel to worship and deeply resented the abolition of services in Kirkbride. Those responsible for the change were looked upon as being guilty of nothing short of sacrilege.

Misfortune and disasters were said to have followed all who had a hand in the destruction of the old parish system and its old kirk.

Abraham Crichton thought little of the ancient kirk and, doubtless thought that destroying it would put an end to the clamouring for services to be resumed. He swore that he would "sune ding doon the Whig's sanctuary". (The Whigs were one of only two political parties at the time and were the equivalent of modern day Lib/Dems. They were also identified with the Covenanters in the late 17th and early eighteenth century and were Hanovarian supporters in the early 18th century. The other party was the Tory party.) So we can conclude that Abraham may well have been a Tory and a Jacobite.

He got some men to remove the roof, but they were forced to stop work by a tremendous storm. Soon after, Abraham was killed near Dalpeddar when he fell from his horse.

His violent end was regarded as a just reward for his actions. There was also a rumour that before he went bankrupt he had dishonestly hidden his money.

After his burial a rumour began that his body would not rest in the grave until he made up for all his wrongdoings. His ghost was often seen in the evening walking in the Kirkyard or grinning over the low wall that surrounded it. The thought of that terrified all who had to pass that way in the dark.

Sometimes the ghost would run after someone unlucky enough to be going to Crawick Mill and chase them as far as the Kirk Syke. That stopped him from going further because ghosts cannot cross a running stream.

People going into town were often chased to the Roddings Strand, a little stream behind the Council House that is now piped and covered over. When held in check by the running water the ghost would make signs as if he wished to speak. No one was brave enough to start a conversation with such an uncanny being, so what secret, if any, the ghost wished to divulge was never known.

In those days it was the custom to milk the cows in the open fields. Often, the gloaming had set in by the time the milk maids had finished their task.

On those occasions Abraham's ghost often made an appearance when the milking pails were immediately flung aside. The frightened lassies, taking to their heels, would run home screaming and tell how Abraham had chased them.

Incidents of that kind became so frequent, and the ghost grew so bold, that after a time, hardly anyone had the courage to pass by the kirkyard after dark. Abraham Crichton's ghost terrified everyone and his exploits were talked about all over Nithsdale.

The ghostly tales were published in a book that sold throughout the length and breadth of the land. Abraham became more famous than he could ever have dreamt of when he was alive. Even some of the most learned men of the day were disturbed by the stories of the ghost.

Things came to such a pass that it was deemed absolutely necessary to take the most drastic action possible to lay the ghost to rest.

It was believed that if a God-fearing man could be found, courageous enough to speak to the mischief-maker and use certain charms that the ghost would be laid to rest forever.

When Abraham's ghost appeared the milking pails were flung aside

A good minister called Hunter, who lived in Penpont at that time, and who enjoyed a reputation for sanctity, was asked to undertake the desperate task.

He readily agreed, and after spending a day in prayer, he went alone at midnight to the kirkyard with sword and bible in his hands and took up his post at Abraham Crichton's grave.

The following morning he was eagerly asked by the townsfolk how he had passed the night. Hunter replied that he had laid the ghost to rest. Abraham, he said, would never trouble them again.

Pressed to tell what actually took place between him and the spirit he replied, "No man shall ever know what passed between us".

Nevertheless, it was said that when Hunter stood at Abraham's grave on that memorable night he drew a charmed circle around him with his sword, and over this no ghostly footstep or evil spirit could pass. When Abraham's ghost made its appearance it was powerless against the man of God. It stood outside the ring and held out its hand to Hunter, who refused it. Instead, he threw his glove outside the circle when it was instantly seized by the ghost and torn to pieces.

With open bible, Hunter completed the magic spell by ordering the ghost never again to disturb or hang about people and their homes. On hearing that command, the spirit gave a fiendish cry and descended into the grave never to be seen again.

Abraham's grave was covered with a large stone to keep him under and prevent his escape. Then a strong iron chain was bound over it and thus the mind of the public was at last put at rest.

For a long time after, local folk had a lingering suspicion that Abraham might rise again. For many years even the bravest needed to pluck up courage to pass the kirkyard in the dark. The fear of seeing the ghost was the cause of many laughable incidents, of which the following is a good example.

During the late Mr Barker's ownership of the Sanquhar coal mines, the pits were situated near Crawick Bridge. The men went to their work very early, generally starting at two or three in the morning during the winter season.

One of the miners called Cringan was a notorious coward who lived at the Townhead and had to pass the kirkyard every morning when he went to work.

On the dark winter mornings, when he wasn't accompanied by any of his fellow workmen, he was in the habit, when he came to the top of the Kirk brae, of shutting his eyes and running down at full speed until he was past the stream between the kirk and the Broomfield. He did this for fear he should see the ghost and, of course, when he got over the running water he knew he was safe. He then took his time and walked leisurely to his work.

Unfortunately for Cringan, he had to go to work alone one very dark morning. The previous day a band of tinkers had come to the neighbourhood, bringing a donkey with them, which had been set to graze by the roadside in the evening.

Tired by the previous day's journey, the animal had laid down to rest on the road in the middle of the kirk brae, exactly opposite the church.

That morning Cringan, as was his custom, closed his eyes at the top of the brae and started running at full speed, when half way down he fell over the donkey. Thinking he had fallen into Abraham's bosom, he got up with a yell and ran off as fast as he could like a madman, till he reached the pit. There he told of his marvellous escape from the ghost, much to the amusement of his fellow workmen who had come the same way and seen the donkey.

Chapter 9
The Ghost House

There was an old house that stood in the field near the bridge at Crawick. It was called the Ghost House, and the field the Forge Park. The field was rented at one time by Mr Rigg of Crawick Forge, but it now forms part of Whitehill Farm.

The Ghost House was unoccupied for a long time, but before it was demolished it had been used as a shed for feeding cattle. The place was said to be haunted by the ghost of a woman, hence the name.

No one went near it after dark and few cared to go near it even in the day time. Frequently those who had to pass that way at night were startled by the ghost of a woman screaming and yelling in a desperate manner. Loud calls for help were followed by a few stifled cries and groans, and then all was still.

Little wonder such a sight struck terror to the uneducated, superstitious folk, who took to their heels, feeling safest when they had got far away from the haunted house.

That was what people believed back in the 1840s. With the house long gone, folk have forgotten the old stories. The tradition was that a helpless woman had met a cruel death in the house and that her ghost visited the place, calling for vengeance on the murderers.

William Wilson, the author of "Folk Lore and Genealogies of Uppermost Nithsdale" never doubted the story. He wrote that about 1880 he was taking a walk to enjoy a fine spring morning when he sat down on the Crawick Bridge not far from the site of the haunted house.

He went to chat to a ploughman for a few minutes whilst his horse rested. The ploughman told him that the previous day he had turned up a quantity of bones and part of what he thought was a human skull. Being curious to see them he was led to the place, which was only a short distance from the spot where the old house stood. There, sure enough were the remains of a human skeleton, but to be certain Wilson gathered up several of the bones in his handkerchief and took them to the doctor for his opinion. He at once said that they formed part of a human body and were the arm and leg bones of a woman.

The ploughman had turned up a quantity of bones

Wilson returned the bones to the place where they had been ploughed up and buried them again.

Mentioning this story to a ninety-year-old woman she replied that when she was a girl she remembered a man and a woman living in the house. They were an ill-matched pair. The woman she said was decent but the husband was a drunken waster who shamefully abused his wife. He also began an affair with an abandoned woman who travelled the country.

Matters got worse for the poor wife with every day that passed. The cottage was situated in a lonely part (it must be remembered this was before the "New Road" and bridge were built) and few people came near the place. Being strangers in the locality they had no visitors and there was no one to help the persecuted woman.

After a time the woman disappeared and when she was inquired after her husband replied that his wife had gone to see her friends. Despite that answer suspicion was aroused and stories of foul play circulated. The man and his mistress suddenly disappeared and were never seen or heard of in the district.

Although no body was found, the old woman said everyone at the time believed that the poor woman had been murdered and strange sights and sounds continued round the house.

Wilson firmly believed that the bones turned up by the plough were the remains of the poor woman who had been so cruelly abused and murdered.

Chapter 10
The dreary Lady of the Linn
(Strange stories of the Orchard Burn)

The peaceful Crawick valley appears to have had a peculiar attraction for supernatural beings. For generations its tree covered glens and leafy braes have been the reputed haunt of ghosts, fairies, witches and other strange beings.

This sweet, rural valley in its nine mile course can boast of scenery unequalled in its quiet beauty. With its woods and waters, glens of hazel and green clad hills it has everything that contributes to making the finest landscape. To increase the charm it abounds in the most romantic tales of bygone days.

Crawick is particularly rich in stories and stirring incidents of the Covenanting times, sufficient in themselves to fill a book. It is associated with some lively doings in the days of feudal strife and the wars with our "auld enemies", the English, and has a wealth of stories of a supernatural and uncanny order.

Crawick Mill has for ages been famous for its witches, and, further up the water, in the Holm woods where the Conrick burn joins the Crawick, is the "Witches Stairs". It's an abrupt crag where the unholy sisterhood liked to hold their revels. Just a little higher, in the middle of the stream is the "Deil's Chair", a rock on which his Satanic Majesty is said to have sat in conference with the water kelpies, warlocks and others of his subjects. But the Orchard with its haunted linn a mile beyond, was, "par excellence" the scene of the wanderings of the troubled spirits of the departed.

The Orchard farmhouse stands on the right bank of the Crawick near to where it is joined by the Orchard burn, a mountain stream that works its way through a deep gorge in the Carco hills on the west.

The Orchard occupies the site of an ancient religious house, latterly the dwelling of the lairds who possessed the land. The apparitions that showed themselves near this place and in the linn were a White Lady and an immense Black Dog. On account of these apparitions the ravine was named the "Haunted Linn".

The "Dreary Lady of the Linn"

The White Lady, known as the "Dreary Lady of the Linn", was a tall, well-made lady dressed in white funeral clothes. It was her custom, at certain times of the year to walk slowly in the evenings along the ridge above the bridge over the Orchard burn and occasionally sit on the bridge parapet.

She was never known to speak to or molest anyone and although she did not shun human beings she took no notice whatever of those travellers who happened to cross her path. She just moved along slowly, ultimately vanishing into space in a manner as mystifying as the way she appeared.

Those that saw the lady said she appeared to be very distressed and her pale face that of a beautiful young woman showed signs of bitter despair. As she moved along, she kept intertwining and wringing her hands as people do when suffering great pain or intense agony of the mind.

Although she interfered with no one, the sight of the Dreary Lady was dreaded by all. Misfortune or bad luck was almost certain to follow soon after for those unfortunate enough to see her.

The story of the Dreary Lady takes us back to the days of the Covenanters during which she lived at the Orchard. She was reckoned to be one of the loveliest of the daughters of Crawick and had lots of admirers among the young men in the valley.

The favoured lad was a young farmer, a God-fearing, good living youth who was well thought of by his neighbours. He was deeply in love with his sweetheart, whom he had known and loved from childhood. Both lovers were looking forward to the time when they could have a home of their own.

Then as now, the course of true love never ran smooth and something or other happened that caused them to break up. Like others who had done the same before and since, the maiden wasn't long in finding another suitor although she still secretly fancied her old sweetheart. By this time he had become a Covenanter and joined the persecuted hill folk, a fact well known to the young lady of the Orchard.

Hearing that her former lover had been seen in the company of another young woman she became so jealous her thoughts turned to revenge.

She got to know that he was about to attend a great conventicle (a banned open air meeting for religious worship by Covenanters) and told her new suitor when and where the meeting would take place. This individual thought if the young farmer, who he still regarded as a rival, were out of the way, there would be nothing to prevent him marrying the love of his life. So he told the military who were scouring the county in search of the rebels, as they called the Covenanters, of the forthcoming open air preaching.

A company of dragoons was ordered to disperse the congregation and in the flight that took place the young farmer was killed. The young lady was shocked on hearing the news and experienced such revulsion that she never again spoke to the youth who thought he had won her over from the farmer.

She became depressed and then turned insane, and within six months of her lover's death her dead body was found lying in a pool in the Orchard burn, her hands firmly grasping a love token given her by him she had betrayed.

The apparition of the Man Clothed in Black was said to be none other than the Devil himself. Dressed in funeral clothes and assuming a pious air, he liked to meet up with people on Crawick road, or join their company in the Orchard linn, or when crossing Carco hill. As he did in the Garden of Eden when he took the form of a snake, he used deceit and cunning to lead them from the paths of virtue.

Her body was found lying in a pool in the Orchard Burn

Money, it has been said, is the root of all evil and no one knows this better than the Devil, who laid his plans accordingly. An easy way to acquire wealth was pointed out to those whom he met. Satan agreed to become the obedient servant for a number of years of those accepting his terms. They were that at the end of the period agreed, the individual who had been served was in turn to give himself body and soul to the Devil.

Success for a while seemed to follow those who entered into the agreement with the dark gentleman, but the end was never a peaceful one. Death came to them in its most hideous form, either in a loathsome disease or in some terrible catastrophe.

However, the old gentleman in black was utterly powerless against those who refused to be tempted by him. Repeating a verse from the bible or a prayer to God was sufficient to chase him away. His retreat was always accompanied by a lot of fire and the smell of sulphur.

A worthy old man called Ledgie Cooper ran a school near the foot of the Haunted Linn about 250 years ago. It was the custom of the schoolmaster to pray every day in the secrecy of the thick wood behind the schoolhouse where he also spent a lot of time meditating. While at his devotions in this retreat he was physically attacked by the Devil who tried to prevent him from praying by pulling at his coat tails. He however continued praying and forced his attacker to leave.

Wishing to teach his pupils the necessity and power of prayer he told them about this conflict with the Devil warning them to remember the promise – "resist the Devil and he will flee from you".

The children didn't grasp the meaning of their teacher and knowing all about the stories of the spirits that haunted the glen, listened fearfully with their hair on end.

Unfortunately the circumstances and old Cooper's peculiar manner were too much for them. They were terrified and believing that the Devil was actually present and standing behind their master they all got up with a yell and rushed out of the school.

It took a lot of persuasion by the old Laird of the Orchard to get the frightened children back. He told them that Ledgie Cooper was an honest man and "it wadna dae for them to allow the Deil, to abuse him at that rate".

The "Deil's Big Stane" is about half a mile up the stream from the bridge. It lies in the middle of the channel and is a huge granite boulder with a peculiar raised band of white spar encircling it like a belt and therefore sometimes called "The Belted Stane". On this rock are some dark purple spots, said to be drops of blood that nothing can remove.

300 years ago a pedlar was waylaid here by a gang of tinkers and murdered for sake of the petty wares which he traded among the cottagers. None of the murderers were ever brought to justice and the spirit of the salesman is said to hover round the immense stone. His death cry, carried on the wind down the glen, often struck terror to the heart and quickened the step of many a cotter homeward bound.

Between the Deil's Big Stane and the bridge was the scene of the exploits of the Black Dog. This was a huge mastiff that would start up in front of those who passed through the linn and with a lot of growling and snarling it tried to prevent them going forward.

It never actually attacked anyone, but when resisted would be transformed into a black bull, or some other animal. Eventually it took on the appearance of a man in his burial clothes and would vanish in a flash of fire.

It was said that a gang of smugglers who had a still for illicit whisky distilling in a secret place in the glen, knew pretty well all that the Black Dog did. They had trained it to prevent people coming near their hiding place and, aided by the uncanny reputation of the linn had little difficulty in keeping up a deception that kept them secure for many a day.

Sanquhar High Street, circa 1912

Chapter 11
Apparitions in Euchan

Euchan Water, like its sister river the Crawick, is associated with many stirring incidents of olden times. It abounds in tales of the Covenanters, and if Crawick can boast of its witches, Euchan with equal pride can point to the elves and fairies who like to frolic and play on its sunny braes.

Ghosts, however, do not appear to have had any particular liking for Euchan Water and stories of the spirits of the dead haunting its banks are vague and fragmentary.

A tall, dark individual who could transform himself at will into a dog or other animal was said to haunt the lower part of the water. A woman clad in white frequented the tree covered banks above the Euchan Falls.

In days gone by there was a fairly large population on the lower portion of Euchan. A village, or at least a decent sized clachan, stood on the south bank close to the waterfall, its inhabitants working in a dye and waulk mill.

Woollen cloth is felted in a process known as fulling. This process consisted originally of beating woven woollen yarn or trampling it with feet in a vat of soapy water. The beating or treading action caused the cloth to shrink evenly as the softened fibres felted together. So if your surname is Walker or Fuller, your family had very humble beginnings!

Water powered fulling mills, or waulk mills as they were known in Scotland, were one of the earliest industrial machines. They are recorded as being in use in France during the tenth century and were probably introduced to England by the Normans.

The felting and thickening process was completed by scrubbing the wet cloth with fuller's earth (aluminium oxide) that gave the cloth good texture and started the bleaching process. It was then washed before being stretched out on tenterhooks (from the French word tentour – meaning to stretch) to bleach and dry in the open air.

The last inhabitants of this long-gone village were two old women who died towards the end of the eighteenth century. They had lived there by themselves many years after the mill had fallen silent and eked out a scanty living by gathering wool and the work of their spinning wheel.

It was said that the constant noise of the waterfall had made both of the women deaf. They were a decent, peaceable pair and regularly attended the parish kirk in Sanquhar for as long as they were able to undertake the journey.

They knew the medicinal properties of many herbs which they carefully gathered and the ointments and brews that they prepared were much sought after.

The quiet, solitary life this humble pair led, together with their old-fashioned ways and their home amongst the ruined cottages of their long-dead neighbours made them seem strange to the minds of younger or thoughtless folk.

Those who preserved herbs a long time ago believed that to get the full benefit of the plants it was necessary to pick them at certain stages of the moon. The old sisters thoroughly believed this and when the moon was in the proper phase they would set out at midnight or in the small hours of the morning to gather the desired herbs.

They often wandered far and the appearance of one or both of the old women at such an unusual time of night may well have given rise to stories of ghosts by those who came across them. That could well be the origin of stories of the white woman of Euchan.

After the sisters died, strange stories circulated in the area, but these, like the clachan itself, are now forgotten.

Many of the ghosts and bogies said to have been seen round Sanquhar were simply the result of the excited imaginations of young folk, who, seated round the firesides on winter nights, listened with awestruck faces to the marvellous tales told by their elders.

These stories had the effect of making even the most stout-hearted feel eerie when passing some lonely place. Any unlooked-for sound or unexpected appearance was sufficient to set the hair on end.

As mentioned, Euchan was a resort of the fairies. The favoured scenes of the revels of these good little folks were the wooded banks at Kemp's Castle, the little holm of Auchenbarran and the slopes above Glenlarie and the Black Hill.

The "Deil's Dungeon", the deep, dark, rocky channel through which the Euchan forces its way in the precipitous ravine behind the farmhouse of Old Barr, is connected with some doings of "Auld Nick".

A curious phenomenon happened at the Old Barr in June 1745. While the farmer's household was seated at dinner something resembling a shower of blue bonnets suddenly appeared in the yard outside. This continued to fall in considerable numbers from an apparently great height.

On rushing out, no trace of the bonnets was to be seen. The household were of course amazed and terrified at such a strange spectacle. This queer sight was witnessed in broad daylight and remains a mystery to this day.

In closing these notes on Euchan the tale of the Ulzieside "brownie" needs to be told.

Brownies were the Scottish equivalent of elves and stories about them were often invented to keep superstitious dragoons from searching areas where covenanters were hiding out.

During the Covenanting times the Ulzieside brownie was a welcome visitor to the farm. He is said to have got through most of the threshing and did much of the drudgery about the place.

This brownie was a much sought after Covenanter who was afraid to show himself during the day. He lay hidden in some secret place about the farm and only ventured out when the household had gone to bed.

Provisions were placed in the barn for him every evening and in return for the food and shelter the Covenanter did all kinds of jobs during the night when no one was about.

Farm Cart carrying line, St. Mary's Street, Sanquhar, circa 1900

Chapter 12
The Ghosts of Littlemark and Dalpeddar

Littlemark is a small farm on the Eliock Estate about three miles from Sanquhar on the right bank of the Nith. The house is surrounded by trees and is a very lonely spot. For many years this place had the reputation of being haunted. The apparition was seen by folk passing near the house in the gloaming, or hazy moonlight. It took the form of a bundle of goods, like a pedlar's pack, moving along the ground a short distance in front of the observer. On going near it, the pack disappeared, or rather got mysteriously less and melted into space.

The story of how Littlemark became haunted begins about three hundred years ago. The house was occupied then by the Graham family consisting of two brothers, Robert and Joseph and their sister Mary.

Although the men were regular church goers and apparently steady, hard-working farmers they were in reality hypocrites and as this story will show, the worst kind of villains.

One dark winter night a pedlar came into the district with a large stock of drapery and other goods, which was carried by a pack horse. One of the Grahams met in with him, and under the pretence of giving him lodgings, took him to their house, where he was cruelly murdered.

Now, Mary Graham was rather an attractive good-looking woman and she had a sweetheart in Sanquhar called Andrew Gourlay. It so happened that on the night of the murder she had a date with her lover.

When Gourlay arrived at Littlemark he was surprised to see the curtains shut tight, which was unusual. Hearing sounds as if a violent struggle was going on inside, he cautiously approached. Observing that one of the window panes was broken, he put the end of his stick in and raised the curtain. To his horror he saw the two brothers, helped by their sister, strangling the unfortunate pedlar.

He hurried home as fast as he could, but said nothing of what he had seen to anyone but his mother. He had cared a great deal for the young woman and he did not wish to expose her. Of course he never went to see her again.

Some weeks after that terrible night she met him at a Sanquhar fair and began to give him a row for not keeping his date. Gourlay foolishly told her that he had kept his promise to meet her, that he had been at Littlemark and then asked her what foul business she and her brothers were engaged in that night. He then turned and left her.

Now all this time the pedlar's horse had been wandering about Eliock woods. No one knew to whom it belonged and nobody bothered to find out. It had been whispered that some foul deed had been committed, but the Grahams felt quite safe as they thought no one had seen them and looked forward to enjoying their ill-gotten gains.

When the sister came home from the fair and told them what had happened between herself and her former sweetheart the brothers panicked, as they were afraid that Gourlay would be a witness against them. The three of them decided to waylay and murder him at the first opportunity. It wasn't long before they set to work on their evil plan.

Andrew Gourlay was a shepherd and was sent by his master with a drove of sheep to a place near Dumfries. It was in the winter and, having a long road to travel it was about midnight when he reached Mennock on his way home.

The Grahams, on the look-out for him at a spot not far from Eliock Bridge attacked him. Gourlay, in desperation, jumped into the Nith, which was in flood at the time. He managed to reach a rock in the middle of the river around which a strong current flowed in to a foaming pool below. It was a dangerous leap that could only be done under the impulse of terror and his cowardly assailants dared not follow him.

He hung on to the rock, but the Grahams threw stones at him until, bruised and bleeding, the unfortunate youth was forced to let go his hold when he sank into the pool below and drowned.

The youth was soon missed and, after a search, his body was found near Glenairlie. It plainly bore the marks of foul play. All his fingers were cut and smashed with the stones and on the rock where he had so desperately clung were found marks of blood and shreds of his clothing.

Gourlay's mother at once guessed who the perpetrators of the horrible crime were and told the neighbours what her son had told her of the murder of the pedlar.

The indignation of the people was aroused and a party set off at once for Littlemark to arrest the murderers. They were too late as they had fled and left no trace behind.

Tradition said that the murdered pedlar's horse wandered about Eliock woods until it died, the people round about being afraid to go near it. The

Gourlay hung on to the rock

body of the pedlar was found many years later by some people who were casting peats.

It was said that many years afterwards one of the murderers, Joseph Graham, the younger brother, visited Sanquhar under the fictitious name of "Beggar Johnie". He was a feeble old man and begging. Recognised at a house he called at, he was accused of being one of the Grahams of Littlemark and a murderer. That seized him with terror, so he confessed his crimes and almost immediately after took a fit and died in great agony.

Mary Graham survived her brothers and returned to Sanquhar parish as an old woman. She lived alone in a solitary hut on the moors and died alone, much to the relief of every one in the district who were glad to be rid of such an evil woman.

If at night a wailing sound is heard to come from the Eliock woods, it is said to be the cry of the spirit of the murdered shepherd.

On the old part of the Nithsdale road that was recently bypassed, about three miles south of Sanquhar near Dalpeddar there used to be a large hawthorn tree by the dyke. It was actually a clump of trees that sprang from one stem and was known as "Lady Hebron".

It was a lonely spot and was long regarded as an uncanny place that was shunned at night by the locals. Those travelling late at night reported seeing the appearance of a lady dressed in white towards midnight. She was accompanied by a child, also in white, which was frequently heard to scream. This is the ghost of Lady Hebron and her child.

The tradition was that somewhere back in the early part of the seventeenth century a man lived near Dalpeddar on a small estate that he owned. He had three daughters who were to share his estate when he died.

Two of the daughters died unmarried, but the third and youngest, whose name was Hebron, married and had one child – a boy.

The husband died shortly after the child was born. Lady Hebron, as the widow was called, continued to live on the property. She lived a quiet secluded life, her whole care being centred in her little boy whom she rarely allowed out of her sight.

It was said that the widow's uncle looked on the child with different feelings, seeing him only as the chief obstacle to him inheriting the property.

After a while the widow and child disappeared. No one could say anything about them, nor were they ever seen again. It was suspected they had met with foul play, but the country was in such turmoil at the time that the authorities took little or no notice of the matter. The uncle got possession of the property without any questions being asked.

That Lady Hebron and her son had been murdered was confirmed years later when the bones of a grown-up person and a child were discovered near the tree bearing the name of the ill-fated woman. The remains, buried beneath a large stone, were found by a man planting potatoes. The woman's skull was split as if by an axe or other sharp weapon. Such is the story of Lady Hebron.

Chaper 13
Evil spirits at the Warld's En'

The "Warld's En'" was the name given to a row of cottages that stood for generations at the west end of Sanquhar, beyond the Lochan. They are all long gone, the last, which stood alone for years was replaced by Rose Cottage, the big house looking down Queens Road at the bottom of McKendrick Road.

The cottages were once one storey high, humble cottages consisting of a "but" and "ben", with thatched roofs. Flourishing roses, convolvuli and other flowers in front of the doors made it a bonnie place.

The Warld's En' no doubt got its unusual name from its position at the very end of Sanquhar town, as it was then.

Many years ago an old weaver called George Ingram and his wife Violet lived at the Warld's En'. One of the two rooms in the but-and-ben was used as a living room while the other was the workshop. It was occupied by a handloom and hard-working George kept the sound of the cheery click of his shuttle going all day long. George was a striking man, tall and well-built and must have been very strong in his youth. By the time this story took place, about 170 years ago, he had become a bent old man whose few remaining hairs were silver grey.

He was a God-fearing, religious, intelligent man with strong views. His wife, Violet Hislop, was a native of Scaur Water where her forefathers had been shepherds for generations.

George and his wife were very superstitious and their belief in uncanny things seemed to get stronger as they grew older. George often encountered the Devil and other imps of darkness.

Often, while he was working they would muddle his heddles. (In weaving, the threads that run the length of the yarn are called the warp, whilst the threads that are passed between them horizontally by the shuttle are called the weft. Heddles were the series of parallel wires or cords in the harness of a loom that were used to separate and guide the shuttle with its warp threads. Muddling the heddles would ruin the pattern of the weave). Other times they would pull his apron or maybe pluck at his hair that protruded from beneath his red Kilmarnock nightcap like a fringe of silver.

In the last piece of cloth he had woven the pattern had been altered three times and many other things were done that could only be accomplished by the power of evil.

His cottage was only a gunshot from the "Fairy Knowe", a green hillock overlooking the "Waird" where Anwoth House now stands. It was called Fairy Knowe because the little folks loved to gambol amongst the waving broom bushes which covered its sides in those days. On Halloween and Beltane nights the fairies lured away the townsfolk's cats and transformed them into little steeds to ride on in their grand processions. George and his wife had seen them, had heard many strange sounds and seen other wonderful sights at the Fairy Knowe.

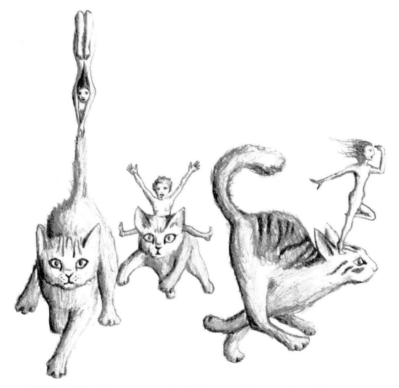

Fairies riding the town cats in their processions on the Fairy Knowe

As said before, George was now old and no longer as fit for work as he had been. He often had to leave his loom for a rest, which he did by sitting with a leg on either side of the little fireplace. He would sometimes doze for an hour at a time with his elbows on his knees and his head resting on his hands.

Now at this time there were two apprentice lads in Sanquhar – Tam Simson and John Hislop, or Pat as he was commonly called. Tom was serving his time at shoemaking and Pat was learning the weaving trade. The two lads were close companions, fond of fun and practical joking. They were seldom together long before they were either studying a new practical joke or carrying out some piece of mischief they had thought of earlier. Their tricks were well planned, and as cleverly executed, so that every now and then the good people of the burgh were amused at some prank or other of the worthy pair.

They weren't fussy about who their victims were and given the chance would play a trick on their own fathers as fast as any others. They were often upsetting someone, but were soon forgiven as their tricks were mostly harmless. If a person suffered at their hands, in a short time he was sure to see some neighbour in as ridiculous a situation as he himself had been.

Tam and Pat were both well acquainted with George Ingram's habits and peculiarities and laid their plans accordingly. One day while the old man was taking his siesta, Tam got a long string with a hook tied to the end of it, climbed up to the roof of the cottage and lowered it down the chimney. Pat meanwhile slipped cautiously in at the back door and attached the hook to George's nightcap, then quietly slipped out.

His night cap was whipped off his head and disappeared up the lum

When all was ready, Pat threw a handful of peas against the window. That woke George suddenly who got up to investigate the cause. On making his way to the door he was further shocked by having his nightcap whipped off his head and seeing it disappear up the lum. Beyond a doubt there were demons at work!

"Violet, Violet!" he shouted, "there is an evil spirit in the house!" Hurrying ben to see what was the matter, Violet found her husband gazing at the fireplace, the very image of perplexity and terror, his eyes staring as if they would loup from their sockets.

"Wi' what ails ye ava, George?" she queried, almost as bewildered as he was himself. "Dreadfu' be't", said he, "the powers of evil are about". He then told her how, while he was sitting by the fire, one of Satan's imps took off his nightcap and flew up the lum with it.

Violet, although not so certain as her husband that the powers of darkness had to do with this strange affair, went outside and had a look round, but no one was in sight. She went round to the back of the house and there she found the Kilmarnock nightcap all covered with soot. That convinced her beyond doubt that either the Devil or one of his agents had played this prank upon her husband.

Tam and Pat were secret witnesses of the scene and thoroughly enjoyed the joke. The nightcap was cleaned, but George would never wear it again. After being, as he thought in such evil hands, he wouldn't even touch it.

Chapter 14
The resurrectionist scare in Sanquhar

Getting on for 180 years ago a great hue and cry arose over lawless characters known as "resurrectionists". They went about the country desecrating the graveyards by digging up bodies that were sold to medical professors for the dissecting rooms of colleges. There was a strong suspicion, not without good reason, that graves were being tampered with in Sanquhar kirkyard.

Accordingly, as in other places, it became usual for relatives of the dead to set a watch over the graves of their friends and to guard them until such time the danger of interference was past. These night watchmen were townsmen, generally young tradesmen, who took it in turns. They were armed with guns and provided with an ample supply of food and drink to keep out the cold and fortify their courage.

There was something peculiarly eerie-like and gruesome in those vigils and the reason that necessitated them that caused an indefinable feeling of fear and apprehension amongst everyone. As the men came off duty in the morning they were always eagerly questioned as to what went on during the night. As far as anyone can remember none of the watchers was ever interfered with. Despite that, there was no doubt that a watch was needed.

When John Thomson, the son of a Sanquhar doctor, was attending his medical classes in Edinburgh he was shocked one day to see on the dissecting table the body of a man he knew well, and who had been buried in Sanquhar kirkyard only a few days previously.

The resurrection business was carried on in quite a wholesale fashion and in some instances with little attempt at concealment. One fine summer day, when the weavers and other workmen had finished their mid-day meal and were standing in groups on the street, enjoying a smoke and talking over the news of the day, a gig with a lady and gentleman drove into the town from the west. It passed down the street and pulled up at an inn at the Townfoot. The man handed the reins to a boy, got out and entering the inn, ordered a glass of whisky, which he drank standing. A bystander passed a remark about the fine weather they were having then and enquired if the stranger had travelled far. He further ventured to ask if he wasn't going to treat his wife to a dram. The traveller replied that his wife never took spirits and, bidding his interrogator good-day, re-seated himself beside the lady in the trap.

Now while the stranger was in the inn some of the weavers came forward to have a look at the turnout as the gig was particularly smart looking and the horse a fine, dashing animal. The lady, who was heavily veiled and with a plaid drawn round her, sat erect in the trap, but the stiffness of her posture caused some curiosity among the onlookers. That increased when the man got in beside her because she didn't make the slightest movement when he got in, but sat bolt-erect, and when the horse made a move fell slightly forward. Then it was discovered that a rope was passed round her body fastening her to the back of the seat.

A shout immediately got up that it was a corpse the man had beside him and a rush was made for the gig. Putting his whip to the horse, the stranger quickly got away and the steed dashed down the street at full gallop with the weavers chasing after him. Further on, others joined in the chase and one man made a bold attempt to get hold of the horse, but the resurrection man got safely away by lashing out at his assailant with his whip. Who he was, or where he had come from and where he was going with his ghastly companion was never found out.

This and stories of other incidents of a similar awesome nature kept the Sanquhar folks – old and young – in a state of timorous excitement for many a day. After the trial of Burke and Hare for the murder of Daft Jamie and others, which took place at Edinburgh in December 1828, resulting in the execution of Burke, terrible tales of "Burkers" and resurrectionists formed the theme of conversation at every fireside. Every now and again the good folks were startled by some of the wicked and loathsome doings of these ghoul-like wretches. This continued for many years.

The stories told about how the Burkers went prowling about at night in lonely roads and on the outskirts of villages. When they met with someone out alone, one of their number would creep up cautiously behind and place a sticking plaster over his nose and mouth. Others were ready with a sack, into which they thrust their victim, who was quickly suffocated. The plaster left no incriminating mark and the body was taken to the doctors and sold to them for dissection.

In those days a nail maker called George Howat had a workshop that was reached through a close. It was a great resort of young and old during the winter evenings to listen to the day's news and the doings of the Burkers were freely discussed.

There was a young tradesman who worked in the shop called James Henderson, but better known by the nickname of "The Skipper". He was a tall fellow, confoundedly lazy and a notorious coward. He found it hard to get up in the morning, so he had to work late almost every night to make something like a decent day's wage. He was an eager listener to all the cock-and-bull stories that were rehearsed night after night in the workshop. He was so interested in these fearsome tales that he would stop work and with open mouth, appear to take it all in. Repeatedly he was told that he should try and get his work done a little earlier, as there was a danger of him being kidnapped some dark night as he went up the close, which was very narrow and favourable in every way for the purpose.

He did try for a day or two, but fell into his old habit again. Fearing that he might be attacked, he borrowed an old sword which he carried with him every night, determined, he said, to cut the head off anyone who should attempt to lay hands on him.

Tam Simson and Pat Hislop – the same worthies who raised the evil spirits at the Warld's En' – were regular frequenters of the nail maker's shop and knew well how matters stood. They resolved to do a little in the burking line and selected the Skipper as their victim.

One dark, wet night, when they knew he would be working late, they procured strong brown paper which they covered with treacle to act as a plaster and waited for their man. They took up their positions in the close and in a short time heard their victim coming. As he entered the narrow part of the close, Tam clapped the plaster on his face, Pat at the same time saying in a low voice, "Quick! Shove him in the sack".

The poor Skipper was immediately in a state of the most abject terror and the sword dropped from his nerveless grasp. He then bounded from them with a yell that startled everyone within hearing and rushed frantically into the first open door, which happened to be his master's, to the consternation of all in the house. His appearance was most ludicrous with his hair standing on end and his eyes glaring and like jumping out of his head. His face, with the grime of the workshop and the treacle plaster made him look more like a tattooed South Sea Islander than a native of North Britain.

It was some time before he could speak, but when he recovered sufficient breath his first words were "Burkers and plaster". George Howat, honest man, examined his face and saw that the attempt at burking had been made by nothing more dangerous than treacle. He and all in the house had a hearty laugh at poor Skipper's expense, who now saw that he had been the subject of a ridiculous hoax and went sneaking home, for once thoroughly ashamed.

Happily there are no resurrectionists or danger of graves being robbed nowadays, but a hundred and seventy years ago the fear was very real indeed and timid people did not care to venture out by themselves after dark.

Townfoot Smithy, Sanquhar, circa 1900

Townfoot, Sanquhar, 1871

Chapter 15
Bryce's Loup
(An incident of the '45)

When in 1745 Prince Charlie raised the standard of his fathers and announced his ill-fated attempt to take the crown from George of Hanover, he got little support from Upper Nithsdale. This is little to be wondered at. The district had suffered severely during the troubled reigns of the Stuart Kings Charles the Second and his brother James the Seventh. In fact, it is questionable whether any other part of Scotland had as much reason to remember the tyrannical reigns of these two despots as had the upper ward of Nithsdale. Its wood-covered glens, moors and lonely hillsides were for years the retreats and hiding places of the persecuted Covenanters.

The martyr's graves, scattered here and there in the district, are silent but impressive witnesses of the part it shared in what has appropriately been called "The Killing Time".

It all began when the Dean of St Giles' Kirk in Edinburgh tried to introduce Charles the First's Book of Common Prayer on 23rd July 1637. An old vegetable seller called Jenny Geddes showed her resentment by throwing her stool at the Dean's head, declaring that she wasn't going to participate in "Papery". Her public act of disgust was followed by the rest of the congregation and soon spread throughout Scotland.

King Charles the First was a monarch who belonged to a dynasty that had several members who were tyrants. He himself was a bigoted puppet of Rome who had no sympathy but rather a supreme contempt for the religious liberties which the Scottish people claimed as a natural right. He went on to fall out with his parliament in Westminster, started a civil war and was finally defeated by Cromwell's army and beheaded. His successors proved equally tyrannical.

The Sanquhar Declarations of 1680 and 1685 commemorated by the monument in Sanquhar High Street are generally considered to have sounded the death knell of the Stuart dynasty.

Richard Cameron, known as "The Lion of the Covenant" and his brother Michael chose the Burgh of Sanquhar to publicly declare a momentous manifesto, the Sanquhar Declaration". On the 22nd June 1680, the brothers, accompanied by twenty horsemen, rode down the High Street, and after praise and prayer, Michael read and afterwards affixed the Declaration to the Mercat Cross, as it was then known. Although there were in fact six Declarations, undoubtedly the most famous was the one by Cameron and this left a mark on the country's history. (A monument to commemorate this Declaration was built over two hundred years later, close to the site of the Sanquhar Mercat Cross, in 1864.)

Cameron and his comrades rode out of the Burgh as sedately and unmolested as they had entered it. They then took to the hills and moors of Dumfriesshire and Ayrshire. The Government immediately became alarmed and military search parties were sent out. At the same time a proclamation was issued, naming those who had accompanied Cameron to Sanquhar and offering rewards for their capture, dead or alive.

At the end of four weeks, on the afternoon of Thursday, the 20th of July, at Airdsmoss, a morass between Cumnock and Muirkirk, Cameron and his devoted companions, 63 in all, were surrounded by dragoons under the command of Bruce of Earlshall.. The contest that ensued was fierce, and a thunderstorm at the time added to the fearfulness of the fighting. The Covenanters fought valiantly and desperately. While only nine of them, including Richard Cameron, were killed, it was said that twenty-eight of their opponents were slain.

When the High Street was being resurfaced in 2006 it was decided to move the monument to a safer position. During building work, a glass container was found inside the monument but unfortunately this was found to be broken, presumable by the vibration of the heavy traffic of the 20th century. The container held several documents but due to having been exposed to air and dampness, all of them were unreadable apart from one piece of paper which had one legible word on it. How strange yet appropriate it is the word "Cameronian"! Several coins and buttons, which were still in reasonable condition, were also found and they are on display in the Burgh Museum.

The Community Council decided to place a new Time Capsule within the foundations of the monument. Many items of interest from the early 21st century were gathered together and put in an airtight sealed container. The container was buried at the base of the Cameron Monument on the 26th June 2006 and a nearby inscription suggests that the Time Capsule should not be opened for 200 years – the year 2206.

How different it would have been had the two last Stuart Kings paid more regard to the freedom of conscience and just liberty to which their subjects were rightly entitled.

No more loyal-hearted men could have been found than the burghers of Sanquhar. Their forefathers had fought and bled at Bannockburn, at

Flodden Field and other stubborn fights. They supported Queen Mary in her last stand against her rebellious nobles at Langside. In addition, the old burgh had sheltered the ill-fated Queen within its walls when she fled from the battlefield to seek shelter in the serpent's nest of her treacherous cousin, Queen Elizabeth the First.

The townsfolk also gave a glorious reception to King James the Sixth when he honoured Sanquhar Castle with his presence on the last day of July, 1617.

Yes, the Sanquhar people were always loyal. Had the last of the Stuart kings been loyal to their subjects, they would have had no stauncher supporters than the citizens of the old grey town and those who lived in the surrounding glens and hills. Because of the cruelty shown by those last Stuart kings only a few Sanquhar individuals flung in their lot with the Prince in 1745.

One of these belonged to a family that had been loyal to the ancient Stuart line. He was Bryce McCririck, son of Homer McCririck from Kirkconnel parish and cousin of Captain Scott, the eccentric owner of Knockenstob. Bryce joined the Prince at the outset, was present at the defeat of Sir John Cope at Prestonpans, took part in the fruitless march to Derby and was under the command of Lord Kilmarnock at the fatal field of Culloden.

After the final dispersal of Prince Charlie's army, Bryce, like many in a similar position was forced to take to the hills. He wandered about for some time in the north, but at last ventured near Sanquhar where he had lived and owned some property. A desire to see his sweetheart, Agnes Corson, would also no doubt influence his coming south.

Afraid to show face in the town, he lay for some days in a cave in the Pamphy Linns, but somehow or other his whereabouts became known.

The Provost of Sanquhar, John Crichton had a long standing grudge against McCririck. In his official position he determined to lay hands upon the rebel and bring him to justice, and thus serve his own private ends under the pretence of a public duty.

Bryce McCririck was a tall, strongly built, athletic man and not likely to be so easily taken, so the Provost got four stout able-bodied men to assist him. He set out early one morning, expecting to catch the fugitive in his hiding place, but McCririck was not to be trapped that way.

He was up early and from the Barr Moor, where he lay hidden among the heather, he saw the approach of his would-be captors. They were coming direct to where he lay and, unable to defend himself against such odds, and knowing that he needn't look for mercy from the Provost, he saw that his only chance of escape was in instant flight. He accordingly rose up and made straight for Euchan water, among whose wooded banks he hoped to evade his pursuers.

The Provost and his men spotted him and all were immediately in full chase. Bryce flew with speed, but was slightly held up when he tripped over a stone and his pursuers quickly began to gain ground on him. Reaching the high bank at Drumbringan, he sped down the brae and reached the waterside.

There had been a heavy rainfall during the night and Euchan was in full flood. In those days there wasn't a bridge. To wade was out of the question, as the force of the current was too great and it looked as if McCririck would be caught. To turn was futile, as his pursuers were now almost on him. Going back a few yards up the brae, he braced himself and took a running leap, which carried him clear over the surging flood and landed him safely on the rock on the opposite side.

Provost Crichton and his men saw the daring leap, but no one dared follow him. Bryce, now in safety, looked calmly across, bade his pursuers "Gude mornin'", and said he hoped they had enjoyed their early walk.

Crichton was terribly exasperated. To lose his prize when he thought it fairly in his grip was more than he could stand. If McCririck could jump the water, why couldn't he himself? Like the fugitive, he too was an athletic man and accordingly he made ready for the daring leap.

Sadly he miscalculated his powers. Instead of landing on the other side, he found himself in the midst of the boiling waters and being carried fast down the stream.

Crichton was truly in a desperate and dangerous plight. His four accomplices were unable to assist him and he was in dire straits when Bryce McCririck gallantly came to his aid. Firmly grasping the branch of a tree, he held out his hand to the enemy and succeeded in landing him safely on the bank.

It would be thought that after this act of unselfish kindness the Provost would have given up all thoughts of making McCririck a prisoner. No, he turned on the man and tried to capture him, but McCririck knocked the ungrateful man down. Soon after that the Provost's allies got across the water and told their superior that they wouldn't be party to anything more being done against McCririck.

Provost Crichton stood ashamed and decided there and then to let bygones be bygones and said he would never again molest the fugitive. He kept his word.

Bryce McCririck was prudent enough to keep out of sight for a while. Eventually he returned to Sanquhar where he lived quietly for many years after. While in hiding he married Agnes Corson of Dalwhat. The marriage ceremony was performed in a cottage among the hills by his cousin, the Rev Alexander Miller of Kilmaurs. Bryce McCririck and his wife are buried in the old graveyard of Kirkbride.

The place where McCririck made his daring leap became known as "McCririck's Loup". When the water is in its normal condition it looks easy to leap across, but when the river is in flood it looks very different and you need to be very daring to attempt the feat.

Sanquhar Council House. (Visit of H.R.H. the Prince of Wales, October 18, 1871)

Chapter 16
Provost Whigham
(How he outwitted the meal merchant)

During the period Robert Whigham was Provost of Sanquhar (1771-1789) there was a year when food became scarce throughout the country due to the failure of crops for several successive years. The seasons had been so cold and wet that the grain didn't ripen and what did was mostly spoiled before it could be harvested.

The heavy tax put upon imported grain, meal and flour prevented the people from getting much relief from abroad. Meal and flour rose in price until the poor public had great difficulty in buying the essentials of life.

Provost Whigham was a clear-headed businessman. Everyone in the community looked up to him because he had the welfare of the people at heart and he was always available for those needing advice and help. He was very perplexed as to how the poor of the town were to get through the winter for the scarcity was beginning to badly affect many families. However, when things appeared at their worst, help came quite unexpectedly.

The Provost was in the habit of spending an hour or two in the evening at the Queensberry Arms Inn. There he occasionally met with travellers and commercial men with whom he loved to chat and talk over the day's news. Newspapers weren't very common then, so a man travelling from place to place was a better source of news than the little papers of the time.

One evening Whigham made his usual call to the Queensberry and sat in his usual place by the parlour fire. The only other occupant of the room was a merchant from Carlisle refreshing himself with a dram after supper.

At that time the whisky sold on the other side of the Border was dearer and of poor quality. Whisky was made in Scotland and heavily taxed when it entered England. The Englishman, pleased with getting a good dram at a low price, was doing ample justice to the "usquebaugh" when the Provost entered.

The two soon got into conversation on the topics of the day. Meanwhile the southerner sipped freely at the drams, which soon had the effect of loosening his tongue considerably. After a time he started talking freely and told the Provost the reason for his journey.

He was in business as a grain merchant and had just received inside information that a sloop, loaded with oatmeal was due at Ayr harbour the next day. The price of meal was still rising, but he expected to be able to purchase this ship load at a fairly moderate figure. After carting the lot to Carlisle he was looking forward to making a pretty large profit out of the transaction. It was his intention to set off early in the morning so as to catch the vessel on her arrival.

The Provost listened intently to all that the Carlisle merchant said and when the latter proposed going to bed, he suggested they should have just one more parting glass. Whigham was at all times a temperate man and on this night particularly so, taking only a small quantity of whisky. He wasn't affected by what he had drunk, but the final glass he ordered was quite enough to finish the Englishman, who with difficulty managed to instruct the landlord when he wanted wakened and had to be assisted to his bedroom.

Before going home the worthy Provost had meanwhile decided his business for the next day. He hinted to his friend Edward Whigham, the landlord, that he needn't be in a hurry to waken his guest in the morning. Reaching his own house, the Provost told his wife about the conversation he had with the grain merchant. He told her he had a plan to outmanoeuvre him by leaving for Ayr at once and try to buy the ship load of meal before his Carlisle friend could get there.

Mrs Wigham warmly approved her husband's scheme, seeing in the transaction not so much a means of profit for themselves but a way to relieve the suffering of more needy and poorer townsfolk. So Mrs Whigham busied herself getting things ready for the early journey. A man-servant was despatched in haste to Burnfoot for the Provost's riding pony. Whigham set off as soon as he got the pony and reached Ayr about eight in the morning. He wasn't a minute too soon. After stabling his horse he went to the harbour and found the vessel he was in search of had just arrived. She had had a favourable passage and her arrival was earlier than expected.

The owner of the cargo was aboard and the captain was anxious to get cleaned out so as to return home while wind and weather were favourable. The Provost examined the meal, and finding it good, bought the whole cargo after a bit of bargaining. He then hired men to unload and secured a number of carters to take it to Sanquhar. In a few hours the whole cargo was unloaded, put on the carts and on the road for its destination with the Provost following at his leisure.

When passing through Cumnock where meal was as scarce as at Sanquhar, the carters had great difficulty in keeping back some of its inhabitants from helping themselves from the Provost's sacks of meal. However, all was safely delivered to Sanquhar and stored in one of the Provost's houses.

To Whigham's honour it has to be said that he didn't take a penny profit. He sold the meal to the townsfolk for much less than they had been paying before. The meal was also of a much better quality than that they had been getting at a higher price.

As to the Carlisle grain merchant. The whisky had taken such an effect upon him that when the landlord went to his room in the morning he could scarcely lift his head from the pillow. After getting a hair of the dog that bit him the night before, he rallied a little, but it was past midday before he was able to set off for Ayr. What his feelings were when he arrived at Ayr harbour and found what had taken place can be easier imagined than described!

Provost Whigham was a true father to the townsfolk. Indeed for anyone to undertake any matter of special importance without consulting with him first was scarcely ever thought of.

During his reign as Provost there came to settle down in his native burgh a man originally from Sanquhar who had amassed a large fortune abroad. He had a great ambition to be made Provost and used all means to try and achieve this, but found it a hopeless task to oust Whigham. He was told of all the Provost had done for the town, and among other things how he had relieved the working population when meal was at famine prices. That didn't stop the ambitious rich man from wanting to fill the civic chair.

At a meeting of the burghers he let it be known that if he were made Provost he would give the town enough money to form a trust yielding enough interest to prevent meal being sold above a certain price for all time coming. This generous offer was warmly applauded and gained him many supporters.

Sanquhar citizens had many faults, but ingratitude wasn't one of them. One of the burghers – John Hunter – rose up and reminded his fellow townsmen of the many acts of kindness done by Provost Whigham. He finished a forcible speech with these words: "No my fellow townsmen, although the rich man should give us meal for nothing, Mr Whigham shall be our Provost, and no other. He it was who helped us in or hour of need and we will not forsake him now". Hunter's speech carried his hearers and Whigham was again re-elected.

Chapter 17
Olden hospitality in Nithsdale

In the "Statistical Account of the Parish of Sanquhar" written by the Rev. William Ranken in 1793, mention is made of the almost continual movement of vagrants through Sanquhar – " a thoroughfare for both ends of the kingdom".

Ranken describes the Sanquhar people of his time as being hospitable to strangers and humane to the distressed. He said that nowhere else in the country was as infested with shoals of beggars. Ranken's concern was that there was no way of telling who really needed charity and those who were simply scrounging. By acting the part and telling some strange tale of woe, scroungers conned simple folk out of kindness that should have been used to relieve the native poor and, "having obtained it, riot in the spoils".

The beggars and tramps of ancient times, or gaberlunzies as they used to be called, had a romantic air about them that was sadly lacking in the tramps of a couple of hundred years ago. In return for an act of kindness, the gaberlunzie was willing to entertain his benefactor with a ballad, or some quaint bit of humour. He was a source of all the latest news and country gossip – always welcome when newspapers were scarce. Unlike the tramps of later years the gaberlunzie was willing to give a helping hand at hay making or assist in the harvest field if needed. As a result, the beggar man was not an unwelcome guest at many farmhouses.

Vagrants in the olden days, on the whole, hadn't such a bad existence. It wasn't uncommon, two hundred years ago for lairds and farmers to entertain beggars with great kindness, giving them supper and breakfast as well as a bed in one of the outhouses. Those of them who were crippled or blind were hospitably treated wherever they went, but at the same time they were a burden on the charitable. In addition to giving them food and shelter, the families relieving them had to carry or lead them to the next house. This was no joke.

Some of the cripples had to be carried from place to place and door-to-door in boxes or hand-barrows. In course of time they almost looked upon the public as their bound servants, demanding such acts of kindness and charity as a right.

In general the cripples were very bossy, frequently foul mouthed and often tremendous actors.

An amusing story is told of an escapade with a cripple in Crawick. He had been brought in his hand barrow to Carco Mains, where he was treated to a substantial dinner by the kind-hearted farmer and afterwards entrusted to two servant lads to convey him to Knockenstob, the next house.

Taking a shortcut through the fields, when the lads were about half way through their task they were alarmed by the bellowing of a bull. On looking round they saw an angry animal about to charge at them and as the bull began to make for them, they dropped the beggar man and ran with all their might for a friendly dyke. Imagine their surprise when the supposed cripple also took to his heels!

More fleet of foot than those who had carried him, he cleared the dyke in a bound and, not stopping to look behind him, was soon out of sight. He didn't return for his hand barrow, nor was he ever seen on Crawick banks again.

Robert Burns

High Street, Sanquhar, circa 1900 showing the Queensberry Arms, also known as Whigham's Inn

Chapter 18
Burns and Black Joan

Sanquhar has been visited and passed through by many men of note, but of all the celebrities, Robert Burns is the one whose visits were most frequent. His connection with the town has made the old burgh hold her head higher and given Sanquhar – "the Black Joan" of his ballad of "The Five Carlins" – a prominence and celebrity far beyond the bounds of Nithsdale.

It was during the last eight years of his life that the bard became familiar with Sanquhar and its people.

At Whitsunday, 1788, Burns took over the farm of Ellisland. As is well known, he had to wait six months before a dwelling house was built for him. In the interval Jean Armour, his wife, to whom he had been recently reconciled, was at Mauchline with their child. As a result, Burns must have often ridden through Sanquhar to and from Mauchline.

His immortal "Of a' the airts the wind can blaw" was composed on one of these journeys, on his honeymoon, as he himself tells us. It was recited for the first time to a circle of his friends at Sanquhar in the Queensberry Arms Inn.

The luxuriant stanzas "Oh, were I on Parnassus' Hill", belong to the same period. It was a long road from Ellisland to the home of "Bonnie Jean" and the tedium of the journey was pleasantly passed away by the cultivation of his thoughts, or muse as he called it.

The Forge at Crawick Bridge, erected fourteen years previously by John Rigg, a Cumbrian, had a reputation for the excellence of the spades and agricultural implements it produced. Burns called there one day about this time to buy equipment and tools for his farm. The manner of his introduction to Rigg is highly characteristic.

The Kilmarnock edition of the works of the poet had appeared in 1786 and the Edinburgh edition in the following year. Rigg had only just got possession of one or other of these books and was deeply engrossed studying it when the bard looked in upon him. Burns at once knew the book and stood silently close by, no doubt to discover by Rigg's expression the effect the reading had on him. Inwardly pleased, he roused Rigg by remarking that: "He seemed deeply interested in the lesson he was taking, and if I might ask, what was the nature of the work that took such a deep hold on him?"

Rigg, looking up, apologised for keeping a stranger waiting and replied that the book was: "Poems by a fellow called Burns", which he pronounced "Booorns". "They're very clever", he said, "and if I had the man here who wrote them I would like to shake him by the hand, and stand him a good drink". Burns thereupon made himself known and over a friendly glass a friendship was cemented that lasted the rest of his life.

Burns' visits to Crawick Forge were many and frequent, and he seldom came into Sanquhar without either calling upon him, or sending for his friend John Rigg. The landlord of the Queensberry Arms Inn at this time was Edward Whigham and Burns stayed with him when his duties as an exciseman called him to the upper parts of Nithsdale. Whigham was a man of considerable literary ability and a close friendship existed between him and the poet.

Regular frequenters of Edward Whigham's house were William Johnston of Clackleith, latterly of Blackaddie and Provost 1790-2, Robert Whigham, merchant and provost 1771-89, Mr Barker of Bridge-end, Crawick, who was the owner of the local coal pits and John Rigg mentioned earlier. All were men of good position who stood well in the eyes of their fellow citizens.

Burns was on terms of the closest intimacy with his circle of friends in Sanquhar. Prodigal in the distribution of manuscript copies of his productions, each of his friends came in for a share.

On one of his visits to the Queensberry Arms Burns wrote the following verse on a window pane in the breakfast room:

> "Envy if thy jaundiced eye.
> Through this window chance to pry,
> To thy sorrow thou shalt find,
> All that's generous, all that's kind
> Friendship, virtue, every grace,
> Dwelling in this happy place.

Unfortunately the pane of glass on which the lines were traced on was taken out of the window frame in the hotel and removed from Sanquhar a long time ago.

"Clackleith" (the poet adopts the familiar fashion of naming his friend Johnston after his farm) is mentioned in the "Postscript" of the copy of that biting satire, "The Kirk's Alarm", which Burns sent to John Logan of Knockshinnoch and Afton, on 7th August, 1789. It is a request that Logan may forward a copy of the "Alarm" to Johnston and is as follows:

> "Afton's Laird! Afton's Laird!
>   When your pen can be spared.
> A copy of this I bequeath,
>   On the same sicker score
> As I mentioned before,
> To that trusty auld worthy,
>   Clackleith, Afton's Laird;
> To that trusty auld worthy,
>   Clackleith."

The conditions implied by "the same sicker score" were that the stanzas were to be kept strictly private. In his letter to Logan, written from Ellisland, accompanying the poem Burns says: "I am determined not to let it get into the public eye; so I send you this copy, the first that I have sent to Ayrshire, except some few of the stanzas which I wrote of in embryo for Gavin Hamilton, under the express provision and request that you will only read it to a few of us, and do not on any account give, or permit to be taken, any copy of the ballad". The "Post Script" to the "Alarm" therefore shows that Johnston was a very particular friend of Burns.

Burns also wrote the bitter "Ode", "Sacred to the Memory of Mrs Oswald of Auchincruive" after a most unfortunate experience in Sanquhar.

In January 1789, on his road to Ayrshire he had put up at the Queensberry Arms Inn. The frost was keen and the grim evening and howling wind were ushering in a night of snow and drifting. Burns and his horse were both tired after the labours of the day and just as he and Whigham were about to eat, the funeral procession of the late Mrs Oswald arrived. Burns was put out of the Inn to make way for the important guests. Poor Burns was forced to brave all the horrors of the tempestuous night and goad his horse Pegasus twelve miles further on through the wildest moors and hills of Ayrshire to the next inn at New Cumnock.

Suffice to say that, when a good fire at New Cumnock had recovered his frozen sinews he sat down and wrote the following ode:

> Dweller in yon dungeon dark,
> Hangman of creation, mark!
> Who in widow-weeds appears
> Laden with unhonoured years,
> Noosing with care a bursting purse
> Bated with many a deadly curse?
>
>   Strophe.
> View the wither'd beldam's face:
> Can thy keen inspection trace
> Aught of Humanity's sweet, melting grace?
> Note that eye, 'tis rheum o'erflows –

Pity's flood there never rose,
See those hands, ne'er stretch'd to save –
Hands that took, but never gave.
Keeper of Mammon's iron chest,
Lo! There she goes, unpitied and unblest;
She goes, but not to realms of everlasting rest!

Antistrophe.

Plunderer of armies, lift thine eyes
(A while forbear, ye torturing fiends);
Sees thou whose step, unwilling, hither bends?
No fallen angel, hurl'd from upper skies!
'Tis thy trusty, quondam mate,
Doom'd to share thy fiery fate;
She, tardy hell-ward plies.

Episode.

And are they of no more avail,
   Ten thousand glittering pounds-a-year?
In other words can Mammon fail,
   Omnipotent as he is here?
O bitter mockery of the pompous bier!
   While down the wretched vital part is driven,
The cave-lodg'd beggar, with a conscience clear,
   Expires in rags, unknown, and goes to heaven.

Mrs Oswald was the widow of Richard Oswald, of Auchincruive who had been an eminent merchant in London. Mrs Oswald died on 6th December, 1788 at her house in Great George Street, Westminster and when Burns was compelled to turn out from his comfortable quarters in the Queensberry Arms by her funeral pageantry, the body was on its way to be buried in Ayrshire.

Another tale concerns Burns noticing a group of boys behind the Council House as he rode out of Sanquhar for Ayr one day. Curious to learn what they were after, he rode close up to them and discovered that the youths had got hold of a rat, which, with a bit of string tied to one of its legs, they were dragging about and poking with sticks.

Instantly jumping from his horse, Burns with a blow from his riding whip, put an end to the torments of the suffering rodent. Turning to the lads he soundly scolded them on their cruel conduct.

"It's only a ratton", said one of the boys. "Ay", replied Burns, "It's only a ratton. But ye maun min', laddies that the same gude God that made you an' me put life as well into that wee beast. Dinna let me hear tell o' ye daein' onything sae cruel again".

Only once does Burns refer to Sanquhar in his poems, and then only by an assumed name – in the election ballad of "The Five Carlins" (witches), where Sanquhar figures as "Black Joan frae Crichton Peel – a carlin stoor and grim".

He is supposed to have given this name to Sanquhar on account of the ancient, swarthy appearance of the burgh. At that time the great bulk of the houses were low, one storey thatched buildings, many of them very old and not as frequently whitewashed as in later days. Crichton Peel, of course, is the name of Sanquhar Castle.

The ballad of "The Five Carlins", originated in the contest, 1789-90, for the representation of the Dumfries Burghs in Parliament. The candidates were the former member, Sir James Johnstone of Westerhall, described as "the Border Knight", the nominee of the Tories, and Patrick Miller, younger of Dalswinton, "the Sodger Lad", who had the support of the Whigs (Liberals).

The doughty rivals are portrayed as trying to ingratiate themselves with the five burghs, which are represented in cleverly drawn, figurative characters – Dumfries, as "Maggy by the banks o' Nith"; Lochmaben, "a carlin auld and teugh", as "Marjory o' the Mony Lochs"; Annan, as "Blinkin Bess o' Annandale"; Kirkcudbright, "Whisky Jean that took her gill"; and Sanquhar, "Black Joan frae Crichton Peel", than whom –

> "Five wighter carlins werna foun'
> The south countries within."

Burns' lines in "The Five Carlins", referring to Sanquhar, show that he recognised the sturdy independence which has always characterised the burghers whom he describes as, "O gipsy kith and kin".

Sanquhar's voice in the election is set forth thus:

> Says Black Joan frae Crichton Peel,
>   A carlin stoor and grim –
> "The auld guid man or the young guid man
>   For me may sink or swim!
> For fools will prate o' richt or wrang,
>   While knaves lauch in their sleeve,
> But wha blaws best the horn shall in –
>   I'll spear nae courtier's leave."

In another version of the ballad the poet becomes prophetic and makes Black Joan foretell the victor. The variation runs:

> "For fools will prate o' richt or wrang,
>   While knaves lauch them to scorn;
> But he sodger's friens hae blawn the best,
>   Sae he shall bear the horn."

The Sodger – Captain Patrick Miller, the Whig candidate, did "bear the horn", for he won the election and represented the burgh till 1796.

In Burns' time there were over a score of ale houses in the parish of Sanquhar. There were two breweries and also a tobacco factory. Illicit whisky stills are known to have been operating within the dark recesses of the Orchard Burn. They were also at the head of Glenairlie, in Euchan and in the Wee Shaw of Glenim, where the last "sma' still" was known to be at work in the district.

Smuggling transactions were briskly carried on, and the caves at Pamphy Linns, then much more extensive than they are now, proved very useful for the storage of contraband goods. More than one worthy tradesman in Sanquhar throve amazingly towards the end of the 18th century and became an important person in the burgh. They owed their prosperity to their connection with contraband dealers who made use of the Pamphy Linns. Burns, therefore, in his office of exciseman had plenty to do about Sanquhar.

Chapter 19
The French prisoners of war and Lieutenant Arnaud

Two hundred years ago, as a result of the long wars with France known as the Napoleanic wars, a large number of prisoners of war were brought over to Britain and located in batches up and down the country. Sanquhar, in common with other towns, had a fair share.

The prisoners began to arrive at Sanquhar in 1810. With the exception of those who left when exchanges took place between the two nations, they remained until the conclusion of peace in 1814.

Sanquhar's allotment was fifty men comprising army and navy officers of various ranks, who were in some instances accompanied by their servants. Their lot as prisoners must have been a singularly pleasant one. They had no military to watch and restrict their movements. Although they were the avowed enemies of our country, they were well and kindly treated by the townsfolk. Beyond certain necessary restrictions as to the distance they might go outside the burgh and the hours at which they were to be indoors, little, if any, check was placed on their liberty.

They were billeted up and down the town. Being in general hearty, good natured and well-educated young men, they got on well with the inhabitants and appear to have enjoyed their compulsory, brief stay.

Their freedom of action was somewhat curtailed when Lieutenant Johnston of the Rifles returned home after being badly wounded at Badajoz. He protested against the liberty allowed, which contrasted strangely with what he had been informed British prisoners received in France.

Being officers, they seem on the whole to have been in easy circumstances. Those of them who kept servants were supposed to be wealthy, but there were still a few who were glad to eke out what means they had. An almost starvation allowance was made by France, and this was supplemented by a grant from the British Government, so if a man had no private income he was not too well off. Accordingly, those not so comfortably situated financially made the best of their time and in their long hours of leisure developed considerable skills in various handicrafts. Nick-nacks of a varied nature, consisting of bone and wood carvings, basket and straw work, and even embroidery were made by them, and purchasers were readily found among the townsfolk.

Well-mannered, young and handsome, it was little wonder that the Frenchmen, naturally gallant, were great favourites with the ladies. The sympathy plainly shown for them as prisoners soon expanded to something of a warmer nature. More than one of the Sanquhar maidens had sad reason to regret her "affaire du coeur" with a fascinating French soldier.

It is easy to understand the jealousies and burning hearts these love affairs would give rise to among the young men of Sanquhar, and to imagine the watchful eyes they would keep upon the movements of the Frenchmen. If any should break parole and trespass beyond the limit – one mile outside the burgh – they would be only too pleased to show their authority by bringing them back within the bounds.

One tough old veteran, who had seen service in the Peninsula and still had fresh memories of the hardships endured in a French prison, also took a keen notice of what the prisoners got up to. He threatened to use the gun he shot rabbits with to shoot any Frenchman who dared to venture beyond the specified distance.

If a prisoner overstepped the limit, his captor was entitled to claim a reward of a pound from the Provost. This reward was once paid to a soldier. Coming on leave to Sanquhar, he came across a prisoner earnestly engaged in fishing on the Nith some miles beyond the boundary. He arrested him at once, brought him into town and claimed and received his reward. If flight was considered by the Frenchman, which is doubtful, the attempt was futile.

Altogether the Frenchmen's lot as prisoners of war was an ideal one. Fond of exercise, they engaged in various games and recreations on the Washing Green and on the Square, and there were some good quoit players among them. Their evenings were also spent in harmless amusements and in all their pastimes they were freely joined by the townsfolk.

One tragic event cast a gloom over their peaceful stay in Sanquhar. Duelling was common in those days and sometimes the merest offence given or taken could only be cleared with blood.

The Frenchmen, as has already been stated, were popular with the ladies. A Lieutenant Arnaud and one of his compatriots were paying their attention to the same damsel and a friction consequently ensued. Their difference could only be settled by blood, so seconds were found and arrangements made for a mortal combat.

Therefore, early one morning a duel took place on the Washing Green. The fighting was with swords. Both Arnaud and his opponent were adept fencers and the engagement was keen. The duel resulted in the lieutenant being defeated and he fell pierced in the side. The doctor present gave the wounded man every attention and he was carefully carried to his lodging, which was one of the houses on the south side of the High Street between the Queensberry Hotel and the Calton Close. Unfortunately the wound was fatal and despite all efforts to save his life he "expired", as his tombstone in Sanquhar kirkyard tells, "In the arms of friendship".

A favourite resort of the French prisoners was the Holm Walks and some of them left their names and initials neatly carved upon the smooth face of a rock which breaks out from the high, right bank of Crawick, close to the footpath. They evidently appreciated the full beauty of that retreat in the wood "Luogo di delizia" that is, "place of delight", was carved by one of them, with the date 1812. There were also the word "souvenir", the faint outline of a coat of arms, the date 1814 and other dim tracings of names and initials that have all but disappeared with the passage of time.

Lower down the water and immediately behind the Holm House, at a sharp bend of the river, was the favourite bathing place of the exiles, and on that account still known as the "Sodger's Pool".

Like all the French, the prisoners were fond of frogs and a favourite hunting ground for this dainty delicacy was the marshy ground near St. Bride's Well.

The French prisoners loved hunting for frogs

Although this ancient well is now no longer visible, as it is has been covered by the railway embankment, it merits a passing mention. The Rev. Simpson regarded the name St. Bride as another form of St. Bridget, an Irish saint, who had nine virgins for attendants. She was held in veneration by the Scots, Picts, Britons, English and Irish. More churches were erected in her memory among all those nations than to any other saint. It is at least a curious coincidence that according to ancient tradition it was customary for the maidens of Sanquhar to go to St. Bride's Well on Mayday, where each presented nine smooth, white stones as an offering to the saint, which correspond in number with St. Bride's nine virgin attendants.

The prisoners were not all Frenchmen as could once be seen from the carvings on the rock, but had amongst them a sprinkling of other nationalities like Poles and Italians. Napoleon, as is well known, having had around him adventurers from almost every country in Europe.

It appears that the prisoners of war formed a Lodge of Freemasons while in Sanquhar. James Smith, author of "The Old Lodge of Dumfries", etc. in an interesting article upon "Extinct Masonic Lodges in Dumfriesshire", says: "The most interesting of irregular lodges formed in the Province was established in Sanquhar". From John T Thorp's book on "French Prisoners' Lodges", we learn that in a sale catalogue of French Masonic books, etc., issued in 1863, stated to have belonged to the library of one of the principal lodges in Paris, there were two items, entitled (1) (Translation) "Historical account of the formation of the W. Lodge of "Desired Peace" at Sanquhar, in Scotland, by French officers, prisoners of war, and particulars of meetings from Jun 13, 1812 to October 14, 1813". It was described as an important manuscript, full of stamps and signatures, and (2) (Translation) "Regulation of the W. Lodge of St. John, under the distinctive title of "Desired Peace", at Sanquhar, Scotland". That was a folio brochure with the manuscript dated 1812. Unfortunately, all attempts to trace the present whereabouts of these books failed.

The proclamation of peace in 1814 put an end to the Frenchmen's captivity and saw them return to their own land. A few, however, elected to remain, some permanently, others for a year or two, where so much kindness had been shown to them. The last living link connecting the French prisoner with Sanquhar was Louis Wysilaski (pronounced Felaskey), who died in 1899. He was the son of a Sanquhar woman who had married one of the officers, said to be the grandson of the last King of Poland.

Stool Clipping at Clenries in 1910

*Jock Murray - one of the best known of Sanquhar Shepherds.
Jock Murray with Glen after winning the "International in 1971"*

Chapter 20
Sanquhar fairs and the local wool trade

Processing wool and making cloth was an important industry in Scotland before the industrial revolution. As mentioned earlier there were at one time at least 120 looms in Sanquhar. In addition to all those weavers, a huge workforce was employed in washing and carding wool as well as spinning it. Indeed the term spinster originates from a time when a large proportion of unmarried women had to spin wool to earn a living.

By the time the Romans landed in Britain in 55 BC they found that the Britons possessed flocks of sheep and had developed a domestic wool industry. Native British sheep were descended from the Mouflon, a small long-legged, goat-like mountain sheep, not unlike the modern Soay, introduced from central Europe by Neolithic man.

The Romans started the industrialisation of wool and by the third century had developed it to such an extent that hard-wearing rugs and capes were Britain's main exports. According to Dionysius Alexandrinus, "The wool of Britain is often spun so fine, that it is in a manner comparable to the spider's web".

The Romans imported their own breed of sheep with improved fleeces compared with those from indigenous breeds. These imports were much larger than the British native sheep and descended from the Urial, a primitive sheep of the Middle East that are probably the ancestors of the Merino. Flocks of imported sheep with fine, white wool were run in conjunction with comparatively large-scale agricultural systems that supplied their settlements, camps and villas.

Towards the end of the Roman occupation a woollen industry started to develop in East Anglia as small farms were merged to keep flocks of sheep that supplied weaving and spinning centres.

Sadly, this embryonic wool industry withered when the Romans left at the beginning of the fifth century and Britain moved into the dark ages, a period of which we have little knowledge. Fortunately, the Romans left their imported sheep behind and these were allowed to breed with the native British sheep.

During the eighth and ninth centuries, the Vikings invaded Britain and introduced their own breeds of black faced, horned sheep that were descended from the ancient Argali sheep of Asia. Those Scandinavian imports are the ancestors of hill breeds like the Blackface, Swaledale and Herdwick.

Britain now had the three principal groups of ancient, primitive sheep in the genetic melting pot, the Mouflon (Ovis musimom), Urial (Ovis vegnei) and Argali (Ovis ammon), and from them would develop the many breeds and crosses that make the British wool clip so uniquely diverse.

Without doubt, it was the Norman invasion of England in 1066, led by William the Conqueror that was the catalyst for a major expansion of the domestic sheep flock. King William reformed the English church system allowing monasteries to flourish. Monastic farming systems cleared trees from the land or drained it, thereby expanding the area under cultivation. The abbeys kept large flocks of sheep and used the wool to clothe the monks as well as the servants and tenants on their estates. As an example, by 1290 Melrose Abbey in the Scottish borders owned 12,000 sheep. In addition to flocks owned by Cistercian monks, there were also flocks owned by their tenants. Sheep were seen as a tool to improve the fertility of the land as well as providing a major source of income through the sale of surplus wool.

As the European textile industry developed and expanded, wool became its most important and valuable commodity. Exports of wool flourished to the extent that it became regarded as currency. When Richard the Lion Heart was taken hostage on his return from a Crusade in the Holy Land in 1194, his ransom was paid in wool.

Monasteries developed such large flocks that they were in a position to enter into long term contracts with foreign buyers, some as long as ten years. Futures trading in wool had become common practice by the thirteenth century! The creation of Bills of Exchange has been attributed to this early form of forward trading.

Jews and Italians followed the Normans into England and helped to build the overseas markets for British wool. Jewish merchants developed such a stranglehold over the London wool trade that attempts to tax it failed.

King Edward 1, the "Longshanks", had incurred heavy expenditure building castles in Wales to help subjugate the Welsh and needed his tax to work. So he made Jews stitch yellow felt badges on their tunics to make them easily identifiable. He then hanged 300 and had a further 3000 heads of families expelled.

Italian merchants had the advantage of acting as Royal bankers and they enjoyed a protected and privileged position whilst English kings were indebted to them. The Italians concentrated on the finest wool and compiled a register of the annual production of wool from English and

Scottish monasteries to help with their trading. Italian buyers had the added advantage of supplying Florentine cloth makers who produced the finest cloth in Western Europe at the time and stipulated that only British wool could be used in its manufacture.

It should be noted that wool from the period was fine due to starvation rather than the result of a successful breeding programme for fine wool. As mentioned earlier, sheep were regarded as "the golden hoof" that improved the fertility of the land. Their diet was not supplemented with valuable cereals or scarce fodder during the winter months and they were left to scavenge over common grazing and fallow fields to spread their muck. Under-nourished sheep fail to develop fleeces to their full genetic potential and yield light fleeces of finer wool. Matters were made worse by the widespread custom of milking sheep.

Only fine wool could justify the expense of export at that time, so that cloth woven from it could compete on quality rather than price in foreign markets.

King Edward 1 was the first to impose a permanent customs duty on exported wool in 1275. It became known as the "magna et antique custuma", or the "Great and Ancient Custom" and amounted to 7s6d (37.5p) on every sack exported, or £123.86 in modern terms. That may seem a trivial sum today, but was a welcome addition to the King's revenue at the time.

The new tax was much easier to apply than others and simply involved collecting payments at designated ports before the wool was loaded onto the ships. As with all new taxes it was unpopular and is remembered to this day in the nursery rhyme "Baa, baa, black sheep have you any wool?"

Gradually Britain changed from being an exporter of raw wool, to adding value to it by manufacturing it into cloth.

Sanquhar had three "Great Fairs" as well as other smaller events.

The Sanquhar Wool Fair was held in July and was the great lamb and wool market of the year and, as it followed immediately after that of Inverness, it regulated the price of wool for the South of Scotland. Dealers attended it and a great number of flock masters all interested to know the latest prices.

A report of the 1875 fair records that "prices ranged about the last year's rates, buyers declaring it was then purchased too dear. The recent heavy failures of the tweed trade had also had an adverse influence on the wool trade.

Wool brokers, commission agents and dealers in dipping materials were present in great force, and there was fair demand for Blackface wool,

Cheviot was not so much enquired for and few sales in white wool were made.

In the 1870s, as much as £100,000 worth of trade could be conducted at one fair. To put that sum of money into perspective, if you use the annual retail price index (RPI) as a measure of inflation that £100,000 would be worth just over £7 million in today's terms. If you relate the £100,000 to the average earnings in 1870 compared to today's average earnings it is worth the staggering sum of £59 million. No matter which way you look at it, the Sanquhar wool fair was seriously big business in 1870.

As it was held so early in the season it was a "character" market where the stock was not shown, but bought and sold by the reputation of the dealer.

In the Dumfries Magazine of 1826 there is a notice of tups being incorporated in the July Wool Fair at which prizes were given for the improvement of the breeds and was probably how the Sanquhar Agricultural Show started. The earliest written record of the show is found in the Dumfries and Galloway Standard of July 23, 1848.

The last Sanquhar Show to be held at Crawick Holm in 1932

Born in the prosperity of the mid-19th century, the show finally perished in the depression of the 1930s. The last show was held in 1932 at Crawick Holm, as had become the custom latterly. It was revised as a "one off" event as part of the burgh's celebrations commemorating 400 years since being granted a Royal Burgh Charter on August 8, 1998 when it was held in the Blackaddie Showfield that lies between the Sanquhar Tiles factory and the Nith.

The November Fair traded principally in vegetables and was known as the "Onion Fair". Prime onions were sold in French fashion, braided on to straw strings, whilst the poorer quality was sold by weight.

At all these fairs, the sides of the main street, from the pump well westwards (Leven Road), were occupied with small stalls and booths. The candy barrow and fruit stalls were the centre of attraction for all youngsters who were eager to be bought treats. Above the din could be heard the cheery and inviting call of the proprietor of the shooting stand – "Fire away, boys! Nuts for your money and sport for nothing". That stall was usually surrounded by a crowd of boys. On the table was heaped up a huge pile of nuts and at the back was erected a board painted with circles and other devices in strong colours, upon which was nailed a group of brass rings of various sizes. It was the ambition of the young sharp-shooters to plant within one of these rings the little dart discharged from one or other of the various matchlocks lying over the heap of nuts. The range was only about a couple of feet and strong percussion caps were the only propelling force used. The smaller the ring into which the dart was shot the larger was the number of nuts allowed, but however bad the shot might prove, a few were given in consolation. The local cooper exhibited a varied collection of his manufactures, from the churn down to the smallest articles used in the dairy and country kitchen. The south side of the street was reserved for the sale of boots, shoes and slippers.

The evening was generally brought to a close by the dancing of "penny reels" at the Council House.

Candlemass or the Herd's Fair was probably the biggest event. On that day, the street was filled with strapping stalwart men clad in home-made clothes, the black and white plaid being universally worn. It was either folded carefully and thrown over the shoulder or worn round the body so as to cover it completely down to the knees, just as it suited the wearer, or as the state of the weather demanded. Each carried a stylish stick from the large stock which he possessed, the making and polishing of which passed the long winter evenings. At his heels was his inseparable companion, the faithful collie.

The Herd's Fair was a hiring fair and after they had made their bargain with the farmers for another term of employment they held a great celebration in the town, though even in drink it is recorded they were calm and civil. The same could not be said for their dogs, and much worrying took place, though it is also recorded that little damage was done.

By the 1930s the herds frequented the Commercial Inn, now called the Glendyne Hotel, most Saturdays. One absurd story from that period involved four "weel-kent, but fu'", local herds who decided to move the Tolbooth back a bit so that it wouldn't obstruct the road.

Taking off their jackets and rolling up their sleeves each herd took a corner and on the count of three managed to lift the Tolbooth and place it on the chosen spot. That was when they realised they had set it down on top of their jackets and had to go to the bother of lifting it again and setting it down on its original site in order to recover their clothes.

That apparently was the only attempt to move the Tolbooth!